THE ART OF KICKING

Ultimate Guide
To Kicking And Punting

ERIC PICCIONE

The Art of Kicking: Ultimate Guide to Kicking and Punting

Copyright © 2021 Eric Piccione

All rights reserved.

No part of this publication may be reproduced or transmitted or utilized in any form or by any means, electronic, mechanical, photocopying or otherwise, without the prior permission of the copyright owner.

ISBN: 978-1-7377748-0-8

First paperback edition 2021

First ebook edition 2021

ABOUT THE AUTHOR

Eric Piccione is a real estate investor, author, businessman, and content creator. Eric currently works as a real estate developer in the Houston area, with personal connections to kicking coaches in the vicinity. If you are looking to get in touch with him, use the links below to do so.

You can connect with me on these social media platforms:

> https://kickersofearth.com
>
> https://twitter.com/kickersofearth
>
> https://www.facebook.com/kickersofearth
>
> https://www.youtube.com/channel/UCH04ag54vx_lXU3NbHrB7AQ
>
> https://www.instagram.com/kickersofearth
>
> https://www.tiktok.com/@kickersofearth

Subscribe to my newsletter:

> https://mailchi.mp/f5752c6de084/contact-us

CONTENTS

Introduction 1
Terminology 7
Form and Technique Overview 9
Field Goal Technique 10
Field Goal Drills 34
Kickoff Technique 54
Kickoff Drills 60
Punting Technique 63
Punting Drills 70
Proper Nutrition 79
Mindset 86
Master Your Mornings 105
Professional
Kicker/Punter Q&A 122
Stretching 173
Warm-Ups for Practice and Games 195
Workouts 202
Tools To Help Kickers and Punters Out 233
Conclusion 241
References 242
BONUS 243

1
INTRODUCTION

This book is the result of over a decade of successes, failures, experiences, life lessons, and thousands and thousands of dollars invested in my personal education. There are many, many people who I would like to thank for the creation of this book.

First and foremost I would like to thank God for blessing me with the opportunity to live on this beautiful planet.

I'm grateful for my mom, Donna, who would put up with me kicking footballs into the kicking net even when it was fully dark out. Her backyard did not look too great after a session and yet she never mentioned anything about it because she knew it meant a lot to me.

My incredible wife, Polina, has always been by my side no matter the situation. She is my rock and I am eternally grateful for the amazing things she does for me. She was a huge part in helping me reach the next level of my athletic abilities throughout college.

Next, I would like to thank my dad, Jim, for catching the footballs when I would practice kicking as a young kid. We would go out for hours and he would stand behind the uprights and blow out a shoulder throwing so many footballs back to me. That "one more kick" mentality is something that he still talks to me about today. Not only was he there for me to catch and return footballs for countless hours, he drove me to every single kicking camp, training lesson, and college visit I ever had throughout high school. If it were just me on my own, it would have been a completely different story and I'm not entirely sure this book would be a reality.

Next, I would like to thank my mentor, Nick Gatto, for giving me the confidence and technical adjustments I needed in order to perform at my best possible level. There are not many men like him in this world, and it's truly a blessing to have learned from someone who is so kind, caring, and optimistic.

There are so many other people whom I would like to thank for their contribution to this book, but you guys know who you are and I thank you so much for all that you've done.

When I started kicking, I was a young sixth-grader with a background in soccer. All I knew was chaotic "bumblebee" soccer: where all twenty-two players would huddle around the ball until the ball then went somewhere else and the crowd would follow as such. So to transition into a disciplined sport like football was quite the mental shift. I played as a defensive lineman and also kicker, because the coach learned that I had a soccer background. (I spent one day practicing open-field kickoffs and they went farther than anyone else, so he just sort of threw me into the position.) That year on the football team I realized I had a special talent for kicker: as all of my kickoffs were going over the returner's head, and this happened game after game. There was something about blasting a kickoff that created a desire to do more of this year after year.

I remember the first day I went out for football practice at Brookside Intermediate School. No offense to soccer players, but I have never actually done any overly physically demanding tasks in any sports prior to football. So when I wasn't sure what line I was supposed to stand in because I wasn't assigned a position yet, the coach made me do up-downs . . . and I started to cry. I was a real tough guy back then, and after practice that day I told my mom I wanted to quit. She told me to persevere and to keep trying at least for another week, and at that point I could then decide what I wanted to do. Thank God she did.

So I played football through Intermediate School as both the kicker and punter and the offensive and defensive lineman. And I loved every second of it. However, when I got to high school in the ninth grade, I wanted to focus purely on soccer. I loved soccer so much, but I realized after my freshman year that I had a much better chance of making it in college if I played football. So my sophomore year in high school I played both soccer and football.

After soccer practice, I would kick footballs into either a soccer net or open field for at least two hours every day. My soccer coach hated it because he wanted me to focus on soccer while I was on his team. I had less playing time as the years went on in high school, since I was more focused on football. But I still enjoyed being around my best friends every day.

I think that's an important point to note: that, throughout your journey, people will tell you "you're not able to make it", "the chances are small", or will just straight up do everything in their power to prevent you from following your passion. Never stop working towards your dream. If it's important to you, you will find a way; if it's not, you will find an excuse.

After my sophomore year, I went to my first kicking camp—hosted by Brent Grablachoff of Kicking World—and ended up winning both the kickoff and field gold portions of the camp. That was when I discovered that I had a really good chance of going to college for football if I really dedicated myself to it. (I also became the first person ever to win all three competitions at a Kicking World camp—field goals, punts, and kickoffs—which I achieved in my junior summer, making me a "triple threat champion".)

After my junior season I went looking for a mentor, and I found Nick Gatto (out of Spring, Texas), who transformed me from just a raw-talent kicker into a technically efficient kicker. In fact, I made such a radical change that I went from winning no awards in the district my junior year to being all-district kicker and punter my senior year, along with all-state academic honors. While it was a massive change from junior to senior year, it took a massive effort to get there. Every day at least one-to-two hours a day I was doing something to improve. Eventually, I was kicking or working out six days a week. But that really is a testament to how important having a great coach is. They can take you from a raw talent to an elite-level kicker if the drive and desire to improve and be coachable are high enough within you.

I still didn't have much interest from colleges after my senior season, so I went to a few kicking camps to get my name out there. I ended up winning the Chris Sailer Vegas kickoff competition out of over three hundred specialists and, on top of that, was ranked an All-American with Brian Jackson's kicking camps. Still not a whole lot of interest from colleges. Finally, I had a junior college up in Brenham, Texas reach out to me and tell me they were interested in providing me with a scholarship. After some back-and-forth thinking, I weighed my options and decided to go to Blinn for two seasons, get some game time and film, and move to a bigger school.

I actually struggled during my time there; but I fully believe that it was because of those lessons that I was then able to become a much mentally stronger kicker at my next opportunity. Two weeks before graduating from Blinn I had no idea where I wanted to go. I had a few schools offer a preferred walk-on opportunity and I was almost set on signing with one of them, but then I got a call from Northwestern State University in Natchitoches, Louisiana. All of the boxes were checked off and I decided to go on a visit during the Christmas break.

On my way up there I was trying to schedule a visit with Stephen F. Austin, another potential college I was thinking of attending, but the visit didn't end up going through. To be honest, it was for the best. Because once I got to NSU, I fell in love with the campus. It was everything that I was looking for in a college and after my visit I signed to NSU, where I ended up setting multiple records and meeting my wife, Polina. Following my graduation I think back and am amazed for what God did. He works in mysterious ways: you may not understand it in the moment, but the big guy upstairs always has a plan for you and where you are headed.

I've always believed that everything happens for a reason and I'm very thankful for my time there as it made me the man I am today.

A lot of coaches in this world are only teaching people who are based in the same region in which they coach. The unfortunate news is therefore that, if you don't live in that territory, you won't get coached by them in person. That's why this book has been created. It is a collection of all the lessons I've gained in my life and I hope to return the favor to you guys and gals.

So rather than your spending thousands of dollars on plane tickets or hours of driving to go to these camps and coaches, I hope to improve your game by at least 1%. If I can do that, this was a success. If you want to find me elsewhere, feel free to reach out via TikTok, Instagram, YouTube, and Twitter @kickersofearth.

The first section of the book will be about form and technique. The second will be about mindset and how to overcome adversity. The third and final section will be all about workouts (there will be strengthening exercises you can do to become a stronger, more explosive, and more athletic kicker and punter).

Lastly, all of the advice put into this book is from practical application throughout my own kicking career. There are a million ways to kick a football, but there are really only a few ways to hit a ball consistently over and over again. And these are the techniques that will help you become extremely consistent in your

kicking career.

WHAT TO DO WITH THIS BOOK

It's important to know that this book is merely a guide: to help you understand, as much as you can, what to be conscious about and what to look for each time you kick a football. As it is very easy to kick fifteen balls in a row and not learn a single thing by doing so.

Hopefully this will be something you will refer back to years after your first read of it: just to check in, and to make sure these are still things that you practice. Don't just read this book—apply it, and work on at least one thing every single day. Grab a highlighter and a pen; take screenshots; make as many notes as you can: all to get the full value out of this book, both in the digital edition and the printed version.

This book is not designed to just be read once. Instead, this should be something that you refer to years down the road as you continue to perfect your kicking and punting craft. Let this provide the answers you are looking for so you can become more confident in yourself and kicking and punting abilities. Moving forward, after each kicking/punting session keep a journal with you so you can track how you felt during your session and can learn from it moving forward.

WHAT TO GET TO START KICKING/PUNTING

If this is your first time ever trying to kick a football, congratulations! You're about to enter a world of crazy precision. There are a lot of little details that have to come together in order for you to make a kick, but after some time this can become one of the most therapeutic and relaxing ways to clear your head.

If this is not your first rodeo, understand that this is not a one-size-fits-all technical approach. I am literally giving out every little bit of information that I've ever learned on field goal kicking workouts and mindset. The aim is to make you a much more confident and consistent kicker and punter. Find some key takeaways, and use them to catapult you into a new level for yourself.

First things first, we have to establish the proper kicking attire. You will definitely need some kicking cleats. It's best to go for comfort over style, especially when your feet are the reason why you're playing that position. Therefore, finding a comfortable cleat like the Adidas Nemesis 18.3 is an incredible way to boost your ability, since you won't have to worry about blisters.

There are hundreds of other kicking cleats out there, but there are very few that have the next level of comfort like the Nemesis 18.3 has.

After you get your kicking cleats, you will need comfortable athletic wear. You must protect your feet at all costs, plus it's not fun having to sacrifice your form in order to make sure your feet don't get blistered further. Therefore it goes without saying that having good, plush, comfy athletic socks won't wear out your feet nearly as fast as those made of rough material. It also works wonders to have clothes that are breathable and stretchy: preferably Dri-Fit ones. You don't have to break the bank in order to buy these, but they need to be comfortable if you're going to be doing an athletic movement such as a kick.

You'll also need a field goal holder, proper footballs, and a kickoff tee. These and quite a few other resources to start kicking/punting can be found at kickersofearth.com/resources/

Enjoy the book!

Eric

2
TERMINOLOGY

STARTING OUT—THE TERMINOLOGY

Kicking field goals can be overwhelming when you first start, but as you get more comfortable with the proper fundamentals, things get a whole lot easier. The goal of this book is to give you a level of knowledge that you may not have ever had, even if you are a beginner-, intermediate-, or advanced-level kicker or punter.

It might be worthwhile to lay down some terminology first, so that we're all on the same page with what I'm referencing when I talk about certain technical adjustments. I will cover all of these terms throughout the book, but some of the most common ones I will use are:

- Staying on your line (staying disciplined on your approach to the ball).

- Lean out (lean your body away from the ball to allow proper leverage to swing up and through).

- Arm high (the arm opposite your kicking leg should be at or above chest height to allow proper body position at contact).

- Counter arm (the arm opposite of your kicking leg. If you are a left-footed kicker, this would be your right arm, and vice versa).

- Being square (pointing your hips and chest at your target at contact).

- Stand tall (without dropping your chest, maintain a nice tall posture at contact).

- Flex the calf (flex your calf to allow proper foot lock position at contact).

- Drive up and through (after you make contact, drive your leg up and through the ball without stopping your leg short).

- Eyes back (maintaining a disciplined eye position after contact).

- Skip downfield (after making contact with the ball, allow your momentum to let you skip down the field).

- Engage your hips (in your ready position, pull your hips in a little bit to engage your core, thus allowing for a proper power position throughout your approach to the ball).

- Go towards your plant spot (bring all of your energy and momentum towards the plant spot, as opposed to the ball).

- Get through the ball (don't allow your leg to swing across the ball; really make it a point to bring your leg through your target zone).

3
FORM AND TECHNIQUE OVERVIEW

We will split this next section of the book into three different chapters:

- First we will cover field goal technique and drills (chapter 4)
- Next will be kickoff technique and drills (chapter 5)
- Last will be punting technique and drills (chapter 6)

The important thing is not to feel like you have to do every single technical adjustment listed. Yet, if you realize you are having trouble with one specific part, make a point to focus fully on what that is, so you can improve upon it.

For example, if you know you have trouble staying tall, don't worry about your body position at contact just yet. Our first priority is to tackle the biggest obstacle currently holding you back from reaching your full potential.

It doesn't make sense to try and do five things at one time and have poor results on all of them. Rather, focus on one thing that you really need help on, and practice day in, day out until you master it.

A true professional is someone who can focus on one task without distractions and who will not stop until they accomplish that task. So, with that in mind, take a mental note of what you believe you want to improve on, and through each section identify the part that will help you the most. That's not to say you can't read the book from front to back, but I would encourage you to prioritize the things you need the most help on.

With that being said, let's get onto the field goal technique!

4
FIELD GOAL TECHNIQUE

FUNDAMENTALS OF FIELD GOALS

There are some basic things that will help you the most when you begin kicking. One really helpful aspect for me is having mental cues as to what I'm trying to do per kick.

The technique that I have used for years has always been a variation of a posture, contact, and follow-through mental cue. What I say to myself varies month to month but the same core principles are consistent. Many people may have different mental cues, but as long as one gives you the most consistent results, why deviate from it? There is no need to reinvent the wheel if something is working for you and has been for a sustained amount of time.

These mental cues can be something like "plant spot, eyes, contact." Or "tall, lean (lean away from the ball, getting leverage), drive." For me currently, it's "arm, eyes, straight through."

WHATEVER YOUR MENTAL CUES ARE, MAKE THEM REPEATABLE AND EASY TO REMEMBER.

THE NAME OF THE GAME IS NOT TO OVER COMPLICATE IT AND OVERTHINK IT.

BACK TO BASICS

The steps

If you ask one hundred kicking coaches, almost all of them will say take three steps back and two to the side. There's nothing wrong with that, but it's never really questioned where it came from; it's just sort of accepted in the kicking community.

That way, it's far enough from the ball: so that you don't feel too close and can get proper momentum through; and it's also not too far away: where you would feel like you were reaching for the ball or getting every kick blocked.

Nonetheless, when you take your steps for a full field goal, take three steps back and two to the side at ninety degrees. It helps if you put your counter arm directly out to your side, as this helps you visualize your side steps.

Every kick is a straight kick, so don't think that just because you're on a hash mark you have to do anything different with your steps or kicking motion. Take your steps directly to the side: because if you go in at an angle less than or more than that, you leave yourself in a position where you're aiming left or right depending on how tight or wide of an angle you are from the ball. Take your steps at a ninety-degree angle from your aiming point.

TAKE NORMAL STEPS

Now, when I say to take steps back and over, that does not mean gigantic steps, nor does it mean microscopic ones. Take three normal steps back and two normal steps to the side because this is typically the most repeatable way of getting to the exact same spot every single time.

REPEATABLE ACTIONS GIVE YOU REPEATABLE RESULTS.

When you're first starting out, take three normal steps back and two over fifty times per day until you get to the exact same spot every single time. For added precision, put a piece of tape where the ball should be; a piece of tape where your three steps back are; and a piece where your two steps to the side are. You should get used to using visual markers to know that you are in the right spot every single time. If you watch a professional kicker, they are almost always going to end up in the exact same position that they were in the kick before (and the kick before that). They have their consistency down so much that you can look at two kicks two months apart and they look almost identical.

As you take your third step back, align your foot to the ball and to the target in an imaginary straight line, and visualize the ball going through the uprights. As you take your steps to the side, take your opposite kicking foot and put it in front of the kicking foot. Pull your hips in a neutral position, get a very slight athletic bend in your knees. This will then be your ready position. Then look at the target one last time and visualize the ball going through the uprights from where you are.

Body Alignment

This one is important. Point your hips, shoulders, and plant foot at the plant spot. This way you don't have to think as you approach the ball. Simply keep your hips, shoulders, and energy going straight to the plant. A common mistake most kickers make is they torque their body to try to kick the ball one hundred and eighty-five yards and the consistency heavily lacks. Stay disciplined on your approach and keep yourself going to the plant so that your body doesn't put you at a disadvantage by wasting movements.

Smooth is repeatable and smooth is strong.

PREVENTING THE TOE FROM HITTING THE GROUND

Everyone is familiar with this feeling: we go in to kick a field goal and our foot touches the ground, causing ball contact and speed to be suboptimal. Here we lose quite a bit of power since our momentum is being reduced just before we hit the football. While there are worse things that can happen during pure swing, which can affect the ball more, this is definitely a commonality between kickers. Therefore, let's address the most consistent factor as to why kickers hit their toes on the ground before they kick the ball—body posture.

Either we are too straight up in the air at contact: where there's no lean out to the side, meaning we have to generate power somehow, and so we tend to scoop underneath the ball. (I've seen plenty of kickers who have great technique but their foot catches the ground and the ball flight suffers. One session, all we did was have the kickers tweak their body slightly—to lean out away from the football a little bit more than they had been used to—and, sure enough, they were hitting super-clean kicks with great technique.)

The second-most consistent body posture reason is our crunching down as we swing. When we compress our body down as we kick, we tend to tell our body that everything needs to go into the ground, and our leg swing follows as a result. Rather, we must fight to stay taller throughout our entire swing: so that we can get better ball contact, height, and power on the kick.

The last reason is often overlooked, but it's something that plenty of talented kickers struggle with. Our shoulder that is closer to the football tends to drop down, hard. When this happens, as we talked about just a little bit ago, everything falls, and we lose plenty of power and consistency on our kicks. So, using a mix of both tips above—we must stay taller in our shoulders; keep them level, as if we are trying to balance a cup of water on each of them; and lean out away from the football more than we have been.

The main thing here is that—if this is one of your biggest weaknesses—you should focus only on this one thing for a minimum of two weeks, and then reassess after that. What that means is that, around your house and during warm-ups, you should be practicing these little tweaks in your body posture so that you can then move on from that and progress to the next level of your technique.

The breath

Breathing deeply is such an overlooked benefit. It might be the fastest way to gain control over a situation that can seem overwhelming. By simply taking five deep breaths, you give yourself the ability to reset and start again.

As you take your steps back and align your target, take a huge breath in through your nose and out through your mouth, then take your side steps. As you get in your ready position, take another huge breath in through your nose and out through your mouth, then you're ready to go. By being relaxed rather than tense, we allow our bodies to swing in their natural state; the form they are supposed to be in.

Stay tall

When we crunch, our chest drops down and so does our neck. This creates a limiting range of motion for the body. If you're a one hundred and ninety-pound kicker, don't you want to get all of that power and range of motion helping you for each kick? It just doesn't make sense to make it harder for yourself to get height on the ball and have a more repeatable swing.

Crunching is almost always an immediate sign that the kicker is trying to kick the ball a lot harder than he or she needs to. Try it for yourself. Drop your chest down and try to bring your leg up as high as you can. Then, from that same position, stand nice and tall, your chest up; now bring your leg up as high as you can again. You should be seeing an immediate difference.

Keeping a taller chest will translate onto the football field, and will see your leg whip through the ball with much more flexibility and a greater range of motion, allowing for higher and more powerful kicks.

Weight distribution

When you get in your ready stance, make sure to stand in an athletic position to be prepared to go the second the ball is snapped. This also helps you be ready if there is a bad snap: so you can run to block or make a play. Ideally, you want 60% of your weight being on your front foot (which is also your plant foot) and the remaining 40% on your back foot or kicking foot. That way you're in the ready position, but not to the point where you're falling over; yet also not so far back that you have no momentum the second the ball is snapped. A good test to see if you are in a good ready position is to get a friend to gently push you on the shoulder when you're in your ready stance, and if you fall over you need to slightly adjust your weight distribution. Personally, I find tucking my hips into my belly button just a little bit engages me and helps me get ready for the kick. It's personal preference, but I feel it's a really good way to get ready.

Lean out

Just as how in your ready stance you want 60% of your weight on your front foot and 40% on your back foot, the same thing goes when you land into your plant spot. You want 60% of your weight leaning away from the ball and 40% of your weight engaged on the side of your core closer to the ball. The reason for leaning away from the ball is it helps you get more leverage on your kick and draws power from your hips.

There is a fine line to leaning out. If you are kicking in a completely straight-up position, perpendicular to the ground, you are using almost all legs, which can limit your power. The other downside to being completely straight when you kick is that your foot position tends to wrap around the ball, because you feel very 'jammed' and close. So that's something to be aware of: if you feel jammed and too close to the ball at contact, pay attention to your lean at contact.

Moreover, if you find yourself hitting kicks that hook and curve after you make contact with the ball, that might also be a sign you need to utilize a lean out.

Try it for yourself: set up your foot at contact on a football with your body staying completely upright. If you lean out just a little bit more, your foot will naturally fall into the right position. Now you can hit the sweet spot of the football with a little less risk since it's not catching the outside panel nearly as easily. At the same time, be careful not to lean so far away from the ball that you're not able to get your hips upfield and skip straight forward—the farther out you go, the harder it gets to keep your momentum going forward. That's why a nice balance between completely straight up and an extreme lean position is best.

That is also where your counter arm comes in to play: to help you balance yourself out, so you can then utilize a little bit more of a lean out and still get your momentum up field. We will talk about the proper lean for kickoffs later in this book. But, all in all, pole drills will be your best friend for getting to feel how the lean should be; and we will cover that drill in a short while, so sit tight. :)

Flex the calf

When working on proper football contact, the simplest way to make sure your foot and ankle are flexed at contact is to flex your calf throughout the entire backswing, contact, and follow-through positions. This will take your mind off of locking your toe out at contact. Oftentimes, when you try to think about something technical—such as having a flexed foot and ankle at contact—there is a tendency to raise the toe, therefore hitting an X-ball (wherein the ball has a slight alteration in spin, as opposed to a normal end-over-end kick). When you simplify it, and just think about flexing your calf out, you get that little extra flexion that you need in order to hit a clean ball.

Try it out for yourself.

Try flexing your foot and ankle out, then try flexing your calf out.

You might find that flexing your calf gives you a little bit more flexion. When starting to use this as your mental cue, it can become difficult to do when you are kicking full reps. That's why I would recommend focusing on it during your no-step and one-step kicks. During your full-approach kicks, slow it down to about 50% speed so you can really maximize the benefits of having a flexed calf. After a few months, you will be a lot more confident in this and it will become much easier.

Get your hips through

Our hips are one of the biggest sources of power and accuracy used in kicking a football. Therefore, when a kicker tends to miss a kick wide (wide right for a righty and wide left for a lefty), they leave weight behind the kick. This means that, at contact, the kicker has not successfully transferred his/her hips into the swing. If you watch a professional kicker in slow-mo: if they miss to the side their dominant leg is (wide right for a righty), it almost always correlates to their hip position at contact and how they transfer their momentum through the kick after contact. Next time you watch a kicker who misses left or right, check out where their hips are pointing both at contact and after. More often than not, misses happen from hips not being square at contact.

Try it out for yourself, swinging on-air for a field goal. As you swing, be conscious of where your hips are pointing as you make contact with the imaginary ball and after you swing. You don't want to feel like a part of your body is pointing to the side. At the same time, don't wrap your body around like a soccer goalie clearing the ball down the field. Keep your body tall, swing your leg to your target, then naturally transfer your weight through the ball.

Plant spot

After the ball is snapped you will then approach your plant spot. As you land to kick the ball, make sure your plant foot is pointing towards your target along with your hips and shoulders. Oftentimes kickers point their entire body at the ball. When they come into land at their plant, they're either pointing their entire body away from their target, or they overcompensate and open themselves up—creating an opportunity to hook the ball or shank it.

If you ever get to a point when you feel overwhelmed technique-wise, then going straight to the plant spot from your ready position will always be your safest bet. This will give you the best and most consistent results when you pair it with a proper foot-to-ball contact and swing-through. When working with a new kicker, this is the first and most important part of what to improve. Equally, in order to be an elite kicker, you have to be able to do the small little things right consistently. Going to the plant spot is one of the most important things.

How wide a plant should you have?

Every kicker is slightly different here, but taller kickers tend to need more room for their plant foot, and will be right around one foot and three inches from the ball.

A good rule of thumb to get your ideal plant foot width is to take your kicking foot, and place it horizontally between the ball and where you will land. This gives you a visual reference for where your plant foot should end up every time. Once you have your plant foot marked, you can then take your steps back.

Being one foot away allows your body to be a good enough distance to avoid crowding over the ball and/or wrapping your foot around the ball. It also helps you generate more power, since you've got some separation. Just be careful about your plant foot being TOO far away from the ball, because then you're reaching for the ball.

A happy medium always seems to be between one foot and one foot and three inches away from the ball.

How deep a plant should you have?

The depth of your plant foot depends on the height of your kicking tee.

If you're a young kicker and kicking off a two-inch block, the toes of your plant foot should be even with the middle of the kicking tee.

If you are in high school, you should be kicking off of a one-inch block and the middle of your foot should be even with the middle of the tee.

And if you are on the ground (college and after), your heel should be even with the middle of the football.

Another great tip to use to work on your plant foot is to practice planting on the white line at the appropriate depth. For example, if you are kicking off a one-inch block and your foot should be even with the ball, use the line as a visual reference to help you land in the correct position every time. The line is both a visual marker and evidence as to what you are doing right or wrong in your technique. Use the line to your advantage!

Foot placement for two-inch block

Foot placement for a one-inch block down to a quarter-inch block

Foot placement for off the ground

The higher up the ball is, the less you need to get under the ball. The tee does that for you. If you find you're getting a lot of spin on the ball on a two-inch tee, it's a good sign that you should progress to the next tee.

And as you approach your junior year, and you feel like you're ready to take the next step, grind your kicking tee in half to give yourself a half-inch kicking tee.

For your senior year, sand all of the studs off the tee to give yourself a quarter-inch tee, which is essentially just a visual marker for your holder. I would also highly recommend spray-painting the middle of the kicking tee, as it gives the holder a visual of where to put the ball when they catch it.

After finishing the football season, the off-season is a great time to start kicking off the ground to get used to the feel of it. Ideally, once your high school sophomore season is done, start kicking off the ground in the off-season.

Do not kick off the ground if you are in high school. The college coaches only want to know that you can make your kicks. From there, they will look at ball flight and trajectory.

What good is it to kick off the ground in high school if most kicks get blocked? This could also be no fault of your own, but because holders, snappers, and/or linemen have difficulty performing their duties at a young level. So give yourself and your team every advantage possible. That way you look good, and the team gets more points.

Use a tee during the season, and kick off the ground when the season is over.

Ball contact

The proper place to hit the ball is the bottom third of the football. So: if you take an entire football and divide it into three pieces you have the top third, dead center, and the bottom third of the ball. Your foot should be hitting the bottom third of the football to maximize height and distance.

If you hit too low, the ball will spin a lot and it won't go very far; if you hit too high, it will be a line drive and not very high.

When you hit the ball with your foot, there is a big bone on your foot called the navicular bone. This is otherwise known as the second shoelace of your kicking shoe. You want to make contact with the ball with that part of your foot, as to find your foot in a position where you're neither using all quad (like a soccer top-ninety shot), nor all groin (like a golf club). You want the happy medium between quad and groin—this preventing injury, while also maximizing trajectory.

On top of hitting the ball with the big bone on your foot, make sure your foot hits the inside panel about a half inch from the middle seam of the ball. Hitting the inside panel (right panel for left footed kickers and left panel for right footed kickers) heavily reduces your risk of a shank. Once your foot hits the inside panel with a flexed foot, your toes won't be able to wrap around the ball. When your toes hit around the outside panel, the ball physically has to go in the direction contact was made. Think about what happens when your foot makes contact on the outside of the ball. The football has to go that way, because physics won't allow it to be any other way. Hitting the seam, outside panel, lifting your toes up at contact, or having your toes make contact before the big bone on your foot are the biggest reasons for hitting an x-ball, pulling the ball, or shanking the kick. Just to clarify, hitting the seam of the football is not recommended since that is not a clean surface. If you hit the seam, the ball compresses a little differently than it would on a clean surface like the panel. It also means your toes could wrap around the outside panel just slightly. Therefore, aim to hit just inside of center on the bottom third of the ball. If it helps you, when kicking on sticks, make a spit mark on where you want to make contact so you have a visual of what to aim for.

Another way to ensure good contact is to think of swinging from the inside panel through the front outside panel. As a lefty this means swing inside the right panel, keeping your leg on its line through the front left panel. This way you make contact with the innermost panel of the ball and keep your foot on its line through the front outside panel allowing you to really get through the ball for optimal contact. Sometimes, kickers make great contact but their foot flicks up at the last second and leads to a flutter in their kick. They often swing at their target too soon. The goal is to keep your kicking hip and shoulder pointed in between the plant spot and inside panel, as you approach the ball, don't rotate towards the ball or target. Maintain discipline in your approach so you can hit the ball in the right spot.

An inconsistent approach leads to inconsistent contact. Swing your foot to hit the inside panel, and finish your swing down the middle towards your target.

Immediately after contact is made, make sure to keep your leg swinging through the ball at eleven o' clock for a left footed kicker or one o' clock for a right footed kicker. This instills good swing habits because the toe can often wrap around the ball at the last second leading to a kick you thought was good but curves heavily. Trust the swing path, hit the inside panel, and finish through the outside front panel. For a quicker way to explain it, think "swing inside out", "swing at one o' clock" (for a right footed kicker) or "eleven o' clock" (for a left footed kicker) or whatever you want that helps you remember. The main thing is to ensure you make good contact with the inside panel and keep your swing going down the line trying not to curve your leg across your body.

THESE ARE EXAMPLES OF BAD FOOT-TO-BALL CONTACT:

The foot is catching all the way on the outside panel. This would be a shank

I'm using all groin here: I will get height, but will get a groin injury in the process

This is all quad and will be a line

drive/knuckle-kick every time

This is perfect foot-to-ball contact

This is the perfect foot-to-ball contact, in-between all quad and all groin

Be efficient

Oftentimes the kicker will find ways for their body to work against them rather than for them. As a result, by the time the kicker comes to kick the ball, instead of their having 100% power and momentum built up, they are more than likely trying to use 60% momentum and build up for a kick.

The term "be efficient" simply means going straight to your plant spot in the smoothest and simplest way possible. This means not slowly edging back to the plant as we approach the ball, as this will throw off momentum and consistency. Stay committed to the approach line and keep your energy, hips, and shoulders going to the plant.

We don't want to bounce on every step—since our energy is going up and down, not out and through. Imagine putting a glass of water on your head. You would try everything in your power not to make the water spill. Pair that with going towards your plant spot.

Keep your eyes where you're going to make contact; maintain a nice tall posture; and drive your leg up and through the ball, straight towards your target zone.

Keep everything level as you approach the ball, then bring your energy up and through the target zone, skipping downfield. We want our entire body working with us and for us, not against us.

Any crunch—where our chest drops, neck drops, or we dip down a contact—is deemed as inefficient. Be conscious about where you're directing your energy. On the same token, your non-counter arm (the arm on the same side as your kicking foot) should stay as close to your body as possible. When you lift your arm behind the body, it causes you to crunch your shoulders, and then your form works against you.

By keeping your arm next to your side throughout the kick, that is one more place for your body weight to get through the ball. Try it for yourself: lift your non-counter arm up behind your back and see how your chest starts to dip down as a result. We want to keep our bodies tall and long to allow for the proper range of motion throughout the kick.

Swing from the ground up

In the same conversation as being efficient, "swing from the ground up" is a great way to utilize momentum on your kick. Think of a plane taking off. It doesn't go a few hundred yards, lift off the ground, come crashing down and then lift up again: because that would be a complete waste of energy and would also cause damage to the plane itself. Rather, when a plane takes off, it starts slow, staying straight. And then, all at once, everything goes up. Kicking works the same way.

When you come in to approach the kick, don't jump into your last step and lose all that momentum you worked so hard for. Stay low to the ground, and transfer your energy up as you make contact. Additionally, when you swing, don't allow your hips to lose their neutral position. Keep them locked in so that your leg doesn't overextend itself in a backswing, causing you to hit the ground or mishit at contact. Rather, as you swing, keep your hips in a neutral position. Keep your backswing low, but drive that energy up after contact.

A great way to think of it is like a rubber band. When you stretch it out wide its ends move away from one another, and then, when you release it, those ends both explode through, back to their point of origin. Replicate that same mindset when you go in for your kick. Your counter arm comes out to your side and your leg moves back—both expanding, moving away from each other—and then they simultaneously snap together, exploding through your target zone.

It's all about efficiency, so don't overcomplicate it. Simply think your energy should transfer from the ground up. A good way to know whether you have a lot of power activating from your glute coming into the ball is that, on your drive step (the step that brings you to your plant spot), your heel should touch the ground or get very close to it. If you're on the very tip of your toe you're not maximizing the amount of power you can draw from your leg. Think of this like a skateboard. When you push off the ground you're not pushing off your tippy-toes, you're drawing power from the heel and from your glute. It's the same concept here: the power comes from the ground up.

Look at the backswing. It's so high up that my timing will be off at contact and my glutes are disengaged

This is much better. I'm in a loaded position and my

hips are neutral throughout the backswing

Keep your hips locked in

This was covered earlier, but when you're in your ready position, pull your hips towards your belly button while maintaining a tall posture with neutral hips. Then, as you go to make contact, make sure you don't disengage your hips, bringing your butt back. You want to maintain a neutral spine throughout the entire approach through contact (the reason being that the hips are where we draw almost all of our power, and so the second we disengage them that's a huge chunk of explosiveness we're losing). Then, at contact, drive your hips forward a little bit so it helps you get that little extra oomph on your kick. Picture it as the same way as when you cough: your abs tighten, and your hips come and scoop underneath your tailbone in the same way. If you couldn't tell by now, I love analogies; and feeling is understanding. Most of the time you really have to feel exactly what I'm referencing in order for it to make sense.

Another great way to feel if your hips are neutral or if they're overextended is to grab your belly fat below your belly button. If it's tight, your hips are back. If your skin is loose, your hips are forward. Play around with it. Bring your butt back, making your stomach fat tight in your hand, then pull your hips forward in a neutral and engaged position. From here, you should have more belly fat in your hand (unless you're 1% body fat, in which case skip this drill!). This is the ideal position of your hips throughout the kick/punt.

This is a great warm-up to do before your kicking sessions. Practice keeping a neutral hip position and hold your lower belly fat in your hands. This will help you feel the proper body position throughout the kicking motion.

One last way to know if your hips are in a good position or not is by simply raising your knee. Keep your feet together and lift your knee as high as you can. Typically, when our hips are back and our butt is sticking out, when you try to lift your knee, it might only come up to ninety degrees. From that same position, tuck your hips in and raise your knee up to ninety degrees again. A much greater range of motion allows for a lot more power and explosiveness on your kicks. Couple that with a consistent swing and you're destined for an excellent career in football.

Look at the ball

After you plant in your plant spot, your eyes should be looking directly at the ball. After you make contact, do your best to keep your eyes on the ball about a half-second longer—to practice discipline after you swing. In my personal experience, the second I lift my head up at contact I tend to twist my body, thereby opening myself up to curving the ball. When you keep your eyes back at the impact zone for just a little while longer, it becomes easier for your hips to stay pointed at your target zone.

Play around with that and see how you feel. Try alternating between looking at the impact zone for one-to-three seconds after contact and looking up immediately after contact. Some kickers prefer to look at where the ball goes straight after contact. I just prefer to control the controllable. See for yourself which you like more.

Swing through your target

This one can be often overlooked—so really pay attention and apply this principle to your kicking technique. When the term "swing straight through your target" is mentioned, it's simply the most efficient way to get through the ball. Imagine a boxer about to punch an opponent; then, right as he makes contact, he pulls back and doesn't follow through. It would be a knockout if that exact same punch were to make contact and then go through the target, maximizing power.

For those who learn better through golf or baseball, apply that same principle to those disciplines. Say, when a golfer hits the ball, they are absolutely going to follow through the target. By stopping their swing short, they are most likely losing consistency in the process. In addition to lack of consistency, simply stopping the body short of its natural swing might also be putting the kicker/punter at risk of injury.

As for baseball, there's a reason why bunts aren't ever home runs: there's no follow-through.

With kicking, it matters even more. In order to maximize height, distance, and power, your follow-through plays a huge part in your consistency as a kicker.

Another way to work on swinging through your target is to draw a straight line with your foot, from the ball, going straight to your target. I'm not saying it's wrong to swing across the ball, bringing your leg across your body, but it sure is inefficient, plus it can lead to slicing the ball away from your target as opposed to driving through it. The goal is to make your mishits still go in even though they're not the prettiest kicks. A surefire way to make sure that happens is to swing through your target zone. Again, some kickers are able to heavily swing across the ball but yet it still goes very far, but most misses hook to where their leg swing is. Ball contact is even more important for the ball slicers.

Windy days are a great indicator of errors in the form. If the ball isn't cutting through the wind, but rather is getting caught or curving fast, make sure you're swinging right where you want the ball to go. It might not be fun, but make sure you're working on your kicks against the wind.

Down-the-line swing path

We will cover this in more detail in the "kicking drills" section of the book, but one of the best drills you can do to work on ball flight and swing path is to set up a ball on one sideline and kick to the other. The goal is to keep the ball as close to the line you're kicking on as possible. The hash marks to the left and to the right of you are going to serve as your uprights, so the goal is not to let the ball get outside of those two hash marks. It will be tough, but it will definitely eliminate that hook in your leg swing. Not only will it help your ball flight, but it'll also help you get your momentum forward as opposed to across, which is another way to lose efficiency and momentum on your kick.

Go downfield

The term "go downfield" gets thrown around often and you hear it if you go to a majority of kicking coaches. Essentially the term is another way of saying "Keep your momentum going to your target after you make contact with the ball". As mentioned above, the point of getting downfield is that it gets both your momentum and energy moving towards where you want the ball to go. If, after you swing, all of your body weight goes to the side, then it's very difficult to have a consistent result from this motion.

Oftentimes the ball will spray off to the left or to the right when we move in resistance to where the ball needs to go. Don't make it harder on yourself to make a kick; swing through your target, and skip downfield to where you want the ball to go. A great way to help you feel how you should get your weight downfield is to have a friend pull your shirt as you do a walk-through of a field goal. Simply put, just take your steps to the plant and pretend as if you're about to kick the ball, maintaining a shirt pull throughout the walk-through. That feeling of energy going forward is how it should be replicated when you physically kick the ball.

See how all my energy went off to the side and my hips are

facing away from the target? That's not good for consistency

See how my energy and momentum is going through the target, finishing downfield? That's what we call efficient!

Tempo

With all things kicking, the more out of control you are the harder it is to become consistent and hit a repeatable ball. When you come in for a field goal, you shouldn't be dang near sprinting at the ball, simply hoping all that speed will help you kick it farther. It's more about precision mixed with force and momentum. When a controlled force mixes with a precise point on the ball and efficiently uses the momentum to get through it, that's a thousand times better and more consistent than uncontrollably running and swinging as humanly hard as possible.

At the same time, that's not to say that you should try to be . . . . as . . . . slow . . . . as . . . . you . . . . can. Stay in control and have a methodical approach to your field goal. You'll find that when you try to swing at 80% power and speed, you'll get a much better result than when you try to grip it and rip it. Not only does going with 110 % speed and chaotic movements create inconsistency, it leads to injuries as well. Be methodic in your approach and have a rhythm to it.

There should be a linear progression in speed on each step. The first step is your jab step; the second is your drive step. Some kickers like to simply take two steps: and, if that's comfortable for them, that works for me. The point is the rhythm should not go from 0–1,000 mph in one step. The first step is your momentum starter, then the second step is where you generate most of your power to kick through the ball.

Recap of Form and Technique

We covered a lot of material, so make sure to write down what you feel would be the most helpful for you. You can go back to it later on to ensure you are holding yourself accountable. Some of the key takeaways are:

Keep your chest tall, so you can allow for proper range of motion.

Stay going towards your plant spot. Everything should be pointing towards that spot. Your hips, shoulders, and feet should all be going exactly where you are going to plant your feet. At the last step, really make sure you are not opening yourself up by stepping back at the ball. As you land to kick the ball, your hips will become naturally square with the target if you stay on your line.

Really dial in on your swing path, making sure it is consistent every time. A repeatable swing equals repeatable results.

If you feel like you're struggling with one specific technique adjustment, make a point of doubling down on that over the next few weeks to ensure you master it. For example, if I know I have a hard time making good contact with the football, I will do everything in my power to focus on proper contact at no-steps, one-steps, and full-approaches. I will kick with my bare feet, do hundreds of pole drills, plus a variety of other drills covered in this book in order to help me master football contact.

Point your hips where you want the ball to go. When you miss wide right for a righty kicker, you typically left your hips back. Make sure to drive them through the target and keep them square at contact, so that you limit your chances of pushing the ball.

Make sure your eyes are looking at the ball when you make contact. Lifting your eyes up beforehand can put you in a position where you might hit the ball just a quarter of an inch off from where you normally would have if you were looking at the ball. Stay disciplined and focus on the sweet spot.

Bring your energy down towards your target. If you go way off to the side after making contact, you typically need to double down on your momentum drive.

Don't forget to have fun! You're way more relaxed when you have fun.

Recap of Field Goal Technique

Don't try to kill it, smooth is strong, trust your swing.

Good technique will make the kick even with a D ball. If you have bad technique, you risk missing even on a B ball.

Swing towards your target and bring your energy and momentum towards it every time. If you need to, do a Justin Tucker skip-through to ensure you're getting downfield.

Flex your calf to have a solid foot-to-ball contact.

The bottom third of the ball is your aiming point. Hit that and focus on it with your eyes.

When approaching the ball, go to where you are planting with your body, not the ball.

5
FIELD GOAL DRILLS

Starting simple

Before we get into the more advanced drills, we'll first cover the foundational drills that every kicker should know. They are the core of any elite-level kicker, and in order to master any sport you must master the little details.

Often, when a kicker is struggling, the best thing they can do is just go back to basics. We tend to overcomplicate kicking and there is no need for it. Simply do the right drills the right way and you will see a huge jump in your power, consistency, and confidence.

No-step drill

This might be the first drill you learn from many coaches. The reason for this is that it breaks the movement down into bite-sized pieces, helping you understand the motion of a kick. It also requires the least amount of movement, meaning you get the utmost repeatability on this drill. Primarily, this should work on body posture, contact, and momentum.

There are two ways to do the no-step drill:

The first is to line up with your kicking foot right behind the ball and from there beginning your backswing, making contact, and swinging through the ball. During your backswing, be conscious about not trying to overextend on the way back. We want to be in control of our swing, not let our swing control us. Maintain a nice neutral hip position, make good contact with the football, and transfer your weight through the ball. After you swing, make sure you pretend as if there were Velcro holding your foot in place, and that you land gently on it after contact. It will feel weird at first, but it's really good to learn how to utilize your body weight during a field goal.

This is the starting position with the foot already at the ball

The second way to do a no-step drill is to set up your plant spot about a foot and a half away from the ball and scoot your kicking foot back a little bit as well. You should want your plant-foot toes to be even with the middle of the football, or even with the back of the football. This way you get enough room and leverage to do this drill properly. From there, take your kicking foot and move it back about one to one-and-a-half yards. Now begin your backswing, but try not to let your kicking foot go above your hips on the way back, and again you want to maintain a nice neutral spine throughout the entire kicking motion. As you make contact, don't skip through the football. Act as if there is Velcro holding your plant foot down on the floor. Simply transfer your weight through the ball, landing softly on your kicking foot.

The reason that you don't skip through is that you really want to get the hang of getting your weight transfer through the ball. By skipping through on a no-step drill, it takes away from the natural swing our bodies have from such a close position.

By keeping our plant foot down for the follow-through, and not forcing a skip-through, we learn to generate the power only our bodies can provide. Since we are not trying to work on power, your contact point, body posture, and weight transfer will be your biggest focus points for the no-step drill.

I prefer this version a bit more, as I can get more momentum on the ball and it feels more comfortable

One-step drill

Right after the no-step drill, we have the one-step drill. This is a great one to do just to get the movement of the kick, along with the swing path. The most repeatable way to do this drill is to take two normal walking steps back and one normal step to the side at a ninety-degree angle.

While keeping a shoulder width stance, you will keep your kicking foot placed out in front of you, farther than the plant foot. There should be no crossover of the feet. They will stay on their own "train tracks" and from the jab step all the way to the landing point, they never cross over one another.

Since both the no-step and the one-step drills have the fewest amount of moving parts, we want to make sure these are the most consistent kicks we have. There's no reason to have a variation in ball flight every single kick for five kicks straight. Focus on the little things and consistency will follow.

Foot-to-ball contact drill

This one needs to be utilized early and often in your kicking career. The optimal place for your foot to strike the ball is that aforementioned big bone on your foot, the navicular bone (the second shoelace on your kicking cleat). It is the bone responsible for when you hit those great kicks.

There are a few ways to practice the foot-to-ball drill. The first would be to get a partner to be on one knee, facing you, and to place the ball firmly against their knee on the ground. From there, get in a no-step position and practice hitting the bottom third of the ball on the inside panel with the big bone/second shoelace of your kicking cleat.

Don't worry, your partner will be able to handle a solid thump on the ball. Repeat this drill for three sets of ten. The goal isn't to kick the ball as hard as you can, even if you don't like your partner. Primarily, this drill works on correct balance; being in sync with your arm and foot; and, of course, proper foot-to-ball contact.

If you don't have access to anyone to help you with this drill, get one of the footballs attached to a pole, hold the pole away from you to where the foot is straight up like with a normal field goal, and practice making contact with that.

SPECIFIC BALL FLIGHT ISSUES

"The ball rotation isn't clean"; "I'm hitting an X-ball"; "Why doesn't my Kick go end-over-end?"

If you find yourself kicking a football and it always has a weird ball flight or almost an X-ball on it, nine times out of ten it means your toe is hitting the football before the sweet spot of your foot does. Essentially, you're hitting the ball in two places; in even simple terms, your toe is lifting up at contact and you need to make sure that you keep your ankle locked out or flex your calf at contact (they both do the same thing). When you flex your calf, your foot naturally locks out, and so you give yourself the best chance to hit a great ball.

I struggled with this for years. I would always hit a really ugly kick, yet it would go through because everything else worked. But then, in the off-season, I made a point of working on it every single day that I could. So every day for no-steps, one-steps, and full-approach field goals, I would go slow enough to where I would consciously be able to flex my calf and hit the ball with proper foot position. I worked at it for months and, finally, I was able to hit the ball with the flexed foot every single time, which took care of my X-ball problems.

That's something to note—if you work hard enough at something for a long enough and you don't give up, great things will happen. You will find you can fix almost anything in your form with enough patience and discipline.

(A side note on this: if there's something that you really want to try the next time you go out and kick, slow it down to about 50% to 60% speed and power to first really nail the technique, and then you can ramp up your speed and tempo as you become more confident with the new implementation. With anything new it takes a while to adjust, so give yourself the proper time necessary to fix what needs to be fixed.)

Barefoot drill

This is a great drill if you find you're not hitting the ball with the proper part of your foot as awesomely as you would like. (NB: This is a more complicated one, so stay with me.) Take off your shoe, and your sock, then proceed to start with no-steps, then one-steps, then full-approach kicks while completely barefoot—so as to force yourself to become aware of the proper part of where to kick the ball. If you tend to hit the ball with your toe, you will learn very quickly that the best and most comfortable place to hit the ball on your foot is that big bone located on your second shoelace. It definitely feels weird at first but it's an incredible way to make sure you're dialed in on your contact point with the football.

Pole drill

Another incredible drill to work on is what is called the pole drill. This is where you take your non-counter arm and hold yourself upright on either a field goal pole, soccer goal, door frame, or anything else sturdy enough to hold you as you lean away. Simply lean away from the pole and focus on hitting the big bone of your foot to the pole in sync with your arm in a kicking position.

When you kick, make sure your backswing is allowing your heel to be at an angle. We don't want our backswing to be straight back: we want it to be reaching back and at an angle with enough torque to whip through the ball. So rather than being all knee and quad when you're backswing is straight back, we are using the quad, groin, and hip by coming in at an angle. Use your full leg on the backswing. Just be conscious about overextending your leg on the backswing to where your heel goes above your hipline, because that can result in miskicks and injuries. Lean away from the pole and engage your core as a repeat your contact point for three sets of twenty-five.

If you practice daily for as little as a month you will see dramatic increases in your form and technique as well as ball contact.

GETTING COMFORTABLE WITH THE SNAP AND KICK

The T-shirt drill

This is a great drill—props to Nick Novak for posting this on his channel. The drill is very simple. Get a partner to get next to a football set up on a field goal holder. The partner will then hold a T-shirt out in front of the football to where you can no longer see the ball;

then—as you come in on your drive step—right before you kick the ball they will move the T-shirt out of the way. The point of this drill is to ensure trust in your technique without seeing the ball. This also stimulates a live snap and hold because you don't see the ball in its set position until you're just about to kick it anyway.

This is a great drill when you don't have a snap and holder because you don't have the luxury of looking at the football already set up. I highly recommend this drill if you have a partner with you.

Steps

When first starting out, a really good drill to help ensure that you're consistently in the exact same spot every single time for your steps is to put tape 1) at the ball, 2) three normal steps behind you, and 3) two normal steps to the side from that point. For added consistency, get a tape measure and measure the distance from the big toe of your plant foot all the way to where your plant spot will be. To check that you are in a relatively good location away from the ball in relation to your height, lay down: keeping your toes at the ready position of where you would be if you were to kick the ball. Laying fully stretched out, your head should be really close to where your feet would be to land. If your head is well past the plant spot, you might want to take slightly bigger steps to get YOUR natural steps where they need to be. Likewise – if you are too far away – you should consider taking smaller, more normal walking steps back and to the side: to prevent reaching on kicks where you are quite far away from the ball.

For a large majority of kickers, their ready position should not be more than three yards away from the ball. It's best to find yourself about two and a half yards away from the ball or closer, while still maintaining a comfortable distance. The important thing is to take standard steps backward and to the side. You should be hitting the same spot each time. From your ready position, take the measuring tape and mark off your spot. Now that you have a spot marked, try hitting the same distance away ten times in a row.

Body posture drills

Everyone has a different body position at the point of contact and that's completely okay. But the important thing is to make sure your body is the exact same way every single time. This is where proper body posture comes into play. Proper body posture allows you to use those muscles necessary to hit a great kick over and over again. The most efficient way for your body to get through the ball is by doing the following:

- Neck and chest are tall and upright.
- Core is engaged.
- Hips are locked in.
- Counter arm is at or above chest height.
- Foot and ankle are locked at contact.

These are some of the primary things to look for at contact to make sure that you're getting as much through the ball as possible. They all have a direct correlation with your ball flight, even at a 1% difference. If your chest or neck crunches down, you limit your range of motion and therefore your follow-through, which affects your lift on the ball. When your core is not engaged you tend to lose control of your swing at contact. If your hips are not locked in, that typically means your backswing will be a little too high and you're trying to draw power almost exclusively from your quad as opposed to your glute as well. (As we get most of our power from our hips and glutes, make sure your hips are neutral from your drive step through contact.) Your counter arm position is almost always directly linked to your chest height at contact; if your arm comes down, your chest and shoulders tend to come down as well. So by keeping your counter arm at chest height or higher, your body naturally stays more upright and swings up as a result.

That's not to say you should over-exaggerate and put your counter arm way over your head, because that can make you drop your shoulder towards the ball, which can in turn cause you to hit the ground and hook the ball. Keep a nice, comfortable, balanced counter arm and increase consistency in your kicks by doing so. Lastly, in terms of the counter arm, you tend to have a better time syncing up your leg lock at contact when you utilize your counter arm. Think of it the same way as a sprinter—if your right arm comes up your left leg comes up in unison: your arm and your leg are in sync with each other. So, if you have a controlled and balanced counter arm, you have more control over your swing as a whole.

For a physical drill to try, the pole drill (as mentioned earlier on the foot-to-ball contact section) will give you a really good understanding of where your foot, torso, and arm should be throughout the backswing and contact point. In terms of other drills for posture, a really good one is to practice a full swing on-air without a ball and either place your counter arm on your chest the entire time or keep your body as tall as possible.

Shoulders back

Another tip to work on posture is to keep your shoulders back: acting as if you're trying to hold a book between your shoulder blades. That will help your body maintain a vertical position. By keeping your shoulders back, you get your body in the right position and you can help yourself stay upright longer throughout the kick. As soon as you get ready in your stance, pull your shoulders back and down, which will help you stay taller—allowing for a bigger range of motion throughout your swing.

Arm behind your back drill

Another way to do this drill is to take the counter arm (the arm that is opposite your kicking foot; so, for a right footed kicker, this is your left arm) and place it behind the small of your back. Now, if your chest starts to drop, your counter arm will prevent excessive crunching of the upper body and you will be able to stay more upright. Therefore you can maintain a taller body position at contact. More often than not you have to feel it to understand it—so try this drill throughout your entire no-step, one-step, and full-approach field goal warm-ups to feel the difference and keep your body taller.

Hand in your pocket drill

This is for those kickers who tend to bring their arms way back behind them at contact. It's not the worst thing in the world to do this, but it does limit your momentum and body posture. A great way to fix that is to put your non-counter arm (left arm for a left-footed kicker, and right arm for a right-footed kicker) in your pocket while you kick. This will prevent you from feeling like you have to reach behind you at contact.

Arm on your chest

As stated earlier, keeping your counter arm on your chest throughout the kick will prevent you from dipping down and crunching at contact. It keeps you nice and tall. This will definitely feel weird at first, but the more you practice it (and the more comfortable you become with things that will make you better), the faster you will progress. The goal of this drill is not for distance, nor should you care as much where the ball goes: it's simply to focus on getting your body posture right.

Eyes on the prize

This is another drill for those who have a hard time swinging through the ball and tend to wrap around like a soccer kick. And it is very simple. Keep your eyes down at the point of contact and, after you kick the ball, continue to keep them down for an extended amount of time. Try keeping your eyes down the entire time and don't even look at what the ball does. Just internalize how that ball felt coming off your foot and whether you feel like you had good posture, swing-through, and ball contact. If the answer to any of those three key points is no, fix it on the next kick.

The goal is to not make the same mistake two kicks in a row. This drill is best done with a partner who can tell you if you made the kick or not, though sometimes simply just filming your kicks and reviewing them after a set of five is more than fine. You need to start disciplining yourself with those little details on your technique that will only make you better. This drill will help tremendously with your awareness of your technique and body.

Oftentimes kickers want to lift their eyes up as soon as they make contact. Sometimes that can lead to their body twisting and improper ball contact. When you come in and your eyes are down at the contact point you give yourself the opportunity to hit that spot way more often because you're looking at it.

GETTING MORE HEIGHT ON YOUR KICKS

Over the crossbar drill

This is a great warm-up drill to make sure you're getting the height necessary on your kicks. Start out seven yards away from the crossbar in the end zone. The goal is to simply maintain good body posture, good contact, and leg swing: to lift the ball over the crossbar without trying to crunch or dip down at contact.

I promise you: the more you trust your swing, the easier things will be. As you get more confident, move up to six yards away from the crossbar; then five; then four. The goal is to lift the ball over the crossbar from four yards away with a no-step. Once you master that, Go five yards away from the crossbar and start doing one-step drills with the same goal in mind. After about five kicks over the crossbar from five yards away with a one-step, go to a full-approach kick from five yards away. Have the same goal in mind, and try not to break down your form in order to lift the ball over the crossbar. Eventually, height will be subconscious for you and you won't even have to think about getting the ball up quickly. It will naturally happen as you keep your body upright and swing up.

Kick over the soccer goal drill

Very similar to the kick over the crossbar drill, this drill takes that one step further. If you have access to a soccer goal, move it up until it's four yards in front of you wherever you are kicking from. That helps you improve your ball flight since you need to clear the soccer goal while also getting enough distance to make the kick. And if you don't have access to a soccer goal, use a kicking net and put that at 4 yards as well. Whatever object you can find that is over six feet tall to replicate a defensive lineman is fine. We are trying to overprepare so when the real thing happens, you are more than ready. Prepare to win so it becomes second nature.

Hit/clear the upright drill

This drill does a few things. Not only does it work on your lift and height on the kick, it also utilizes your leg swing, accuracy, and consistency. It is very simple: set up in the back of the end zone on the same line that the uprights are on. The goals of the drill are to work on your swing path; to keep the ball on a straight line for longer; and to work on aiming small (so that, if you miss, you miss small). The best result you can have on this drill is a kick that goes directly over both uprights, straight down the line, and does not deviate from the line. That is definitely the hardest one to pull off: but, more often than not, if you hit the upright then that's still a really good sign.

As you get more advanced, start to take one-yard increments closer to the upright after each successful kick that clears the post. The goal is to get at least halfway between the sidelines and the upright, whereby you're still hitting the very top of or over the uprights. That means you are more than capable of clearing a defender from seven to eight yards away. It can also be a great game to play with your other kicking buddies: seeing who can hit the upright the most times, or who can kick it completely over.

ACCURACY DRILLS

Line drill

This drill is very simple, but it can yield so many different benefits. Set up a ball right on the sideline, facing the other sideline. The goal of this drill is to keep the ball as close to the line as possible. By doing this, you will subconsciously work on your swing path, improving your accuracy. On top of honing swing path and accuracy, the more you use this drill the more you will eliminate the curve on your kicks. Not only do you have a visual reference of the line, which goes all the way down the field, but you can also use the hash marks to your left and right as arena uprights to keep the ball between on a kick.

The term "aim small, miss small" is perfect here. Your aiming point is the line, but, if you happen to miss, your next biggest target will be the hashes to the left and right of you. That's the beauty of this drill: you give yourself multiple things to work on simply by kicking down a line. If you had to choose only one drill to maximize accuracy, it would involve kicking on a line to your target.

Foot Preservation Drill

To add to the line drill is the foot preservation drill. Get on a line and set your foot up as if you were to make contact with an imaginary ball. Your foot and ankle should be flexed out. (Flex the calf to get the proper foot position) Now from your contact spot, do not backswing but keep that locked out position and swing slow and controlled up the line about a yard in front of you. You should be swinging in slow motion to make sure your foot is maintaining proper position. This holds your foot angle and prevents you from rotating your foot as you make contact so you have a more consistent kick. Kickers will sometimes rotate their foot as soon as they make contact which causes the ball to hook or slice off their foot. If you have ever kicked a field goal that felt great, but curved really hard right after you kicked it, this drill will work wonders for you.

Keeping your foot down on its line will increase consistency and accuracy. Imagine if a golfer rotated his club head immediately after he hit the ball, the accuracy would be all over the place! Keep your foot down the line and do not curl or wrap your toes in like a soccer top ninety shot. Your foot should look the same at contact as it does after swinging forward a yard down the line. Same foot and ankle lock. Then after keeping your foot locked out a yard up the line with your swing, do it again. Be careful not to let your groin be the only part of your foot that is keeping your leg up. Likewise with your quad. Make sure when doing this drill, you are using both your quad and groin to keep your leg up. If your body starts to favor one muscle group over the other, you're swinging too high. Prevent injury here by using proper positioning with your foot. Another way to think about using your leg is have a happy medium between your knee pointing directly to your side (groin) and straight in front of you (quad) The knee should be right in between those two positions. After you do ten total slow and controlled reps, take a break and repeat for five total sets of ten reps.

Angle drill

This is another great drill for working on your precision. Simply start at the corner of the end zone, face the uprights, and try to kick the ball in between them. Since the angle is a lot smaller than you're used to, this works on keeping the ball flight straight and true, as well as staying calm—even in a less-than-normal situation. Once you make the kick, move up one yard in the end zone. You continue this process, going one yard deeper each time, until you are all the way in the back of the end zone.

In order to work on staying uncomfortable, go to the other side of the end zone and repeat the same process from the opposite corner. If you miss a kick, back up a yard. (So, if you are eight yards into the end zone and you miss, go seven yards into the end zone.) For added difficulty, try making three kicks in a row; and, after that, scoot up one yard until you get to the back of the end zone, then go to the other sideline. Again this is a great drill to do with friends to see who the more consistent kicker is from weird angles. The goal is to get comfortable being uncomfortable.

The horseshoe

This is a great drill for very realistic kicking situations, and it works on kicks from all over the field. It's actually quite simple: you start on one side of the field and you cross it in a horseshoe pattern: moving away from the uprights, and ending up in the same spot on the opposite hash mark. Your setup is going to be this:

For junior high and freshman kickers, your horseshoe drill will start at the 15-yard line on the left hash or a 25-yard field goal. (Whatever the number is, just take off ten yards and that's the yard line the ball will go on.)

HERE'S THE ROUTINE:

25 L (15-yard line).

22 L (12-yard line).

20 M.
23 R.
25 R.
28 R.
32 R.
35 M.
33 L.
30 L.

For sophomores and juniors:
33 L.
25 L.
20 M.
28 R.
32 R.
35 R.
38 R.
42 M.
38 L.
35 L.

For high school varsity/college/pros, your markers will be:
33 L.
25 L.
30 R.
35 R.
39 R.
43 R.
47 M.

52 M.

44 L.

38 L.

This is a great drill, since it works on the hashes at various distances all over the field. As you can tell, these kicks aren't going past a fifty-two-yard field goal. The reasoning is it's very rare to find yourself in a situation where you're kicking more than a fifty-two-yard field goal. As a result, get very comfortable kicking from the hashes and weird parts of the field. Some of the hardest kicks to make for some kickers are the short-distance angle kicks. They are so easy they're hard.

Simulating game drills

Create an itinerary

This drill can be for any kicker, but it's even more beneficial to kickers who are having trouble in games. Take a look at the practice routine throughout the week. Oftentimes the kicker will go and kick for maybe thirty minutes and call it a day. It's important to treat them as a starter, as opposed to a closer. Closers are only good for a short timespan and then their leg starts to give out. Starters are good for the entirety of the game. It's very easy for a kicker to condition their leg for thirty- to forty-five-minute time frames and then they are done for the day. Make sure when the kicker goes to practice, it's not, "Take the footballs, go to the other field, and go home whenever you feel like it."

If you have access to a snapper and a holder, they all need to be practicing game-time situations. So set up a few different itineraries to practice on their own. For example:

Kickoff is at 12:00.

We got an interception at 12:13 and ran it in for a touchdown. Go kick the extra point and then kickoff.

At 12:29 we scored a touchdown, go kick the extra point.

There was a penalty on the offense, so kick the extra point five yards back from the normal location, then kickoff.

At 12:47 the offense got stopped at the 21-yard line. Attempt a field goal from the right hash for a thirty-eight-yard field goal, then go kickoff deep right.

These are just a few of the examples you can try as a kicker. You want to make it as realistic as possible, though definitely throw in some worst-case scenarios. Something like:

Forgot the field goal tee. The kicker needs to kick off the ground for the field goal.

The clock is running, kick a thirty-two-yard field goal on the left hash in ten seconds.

The more scenarios you come up with, the more prepared your kicker will become, game-time. How do you expect to improve if you're not working in any and all situations that can and most likely will happen during the game?

Op-time drills

You most definitely should be working on your op time with your snapper and holder. The common question I get often is, "When should I approach the ball during live reps?"

The average time for an NFL kicker op time (operation time) is 1.2 to 1.25 seconds. That means the moment the ball is snapped to when the ball is kicked is 1.25 seconds. College is right around 1.3. High school is 1.35, typically. (On the higher side, it might be around 1.4.)

There are three main clear points as to when you can recognize your time to go. The first is when the ball is snapped; the second is when the holder lifts his hand off the ground; the third is when the holder catches the ball.

Faster doesn't always mean better, because it could throw off your timing—so you might just have to find the sweet spot that works for you and your team based on the skill set that everyone has. For example, if my snapper has a hard time getting it back to the holder, I might have to adjust my approach time to the second I see any movement on the ball. However, if you have a great snapper who zings it back there, you might even be able to go the second the holder catches the ball.

In reality, though, nobody's focusing on that exact timing: because our reactions are slower than what's actually going on in real-time. So, instead of thinking "I have to go the precise moment his hand comes off the ground", go just a split second after the ball is snapped. And don't beat yourself up over a bad op time: it's just a work in progress. But you do need to get with your holder and snapper and work on that, so that you get more comfortable with game speed.

Last-second drill

This is a really fun drill that can be done to get used to no time-outs remaining, the play clock running out, and your only having a few seconds to run out to the spot and get set up quickly. From there, trust your swing to knock it through the uprights.

There are a few ways to get ready quickly, but the most important thing is to stay calm when you're doing a last-second field goal. In a perfect world, you would get out to your spot, and take your three steps back and over a little faster than you normally would—as that will put you in the best possible position to succeed (i.e. since you are set up in the same position you normally are, this would represent the best-case scenario).

The other way is to go directly where the plant spot is, and go three steps back at a forty-five-degree angle to reach the general location of where you normally are. This is if you have even less time to take three back and two over. It is the same concept here: you stay calm, breathe, go straight to the plant spot, and swing through your target zone.

The final way to do a last-second field goal is to run out immediately to your ready position and make a very educated guess as to where you normally stand when you take three steps back and two over. It's the least consistent (and hence the last recommended) method because it's simply the hardest to replicate time after time. However, if you only have a limited amount of time on the clock, this might be your best option. Since we don't have enough time to do our full line up, everything else stays the same. The main thing is to take a huge deep breath in your ready position and trust your approach line and swing.

Artificial adrenaline, or nerves

When kicking on your own with a field goal holder, it can take you away from what a game-time situation really feels like. You don't really have any adrenaline when you kick field goals on your own, and that's why you will have to use artificial adrenaline to replicate a game situation. Essentially this means doing something to make your heart rate increase prior to a kick.

Some great examples of this would be to do, before kicking, either ten burpees, a twenty-five-yard sprint, ten jump squats, or twenty-five high knees. Whatever you do, dial it to where your heartbeat is elevated and your mind is racing a little bit more than it normally is: so that you have the opportunity to really focus on your breath and trust your technique. The main point is the farther you can get from your comfort zone, the more confident of a kicker you will be—and thus a more successful kicker. Always work on pushing your limits and barriers as a kicker to become the best version of yourself that you can be. Your future self will thank you. Give yourself the gift of growth.

Practice routine and game-day kicking warm-up routine

While practice and game days have two different intentions, make sure you have a core set of kicking drills you do before you're ready to rock and roll. Some of the most beneficial drills are going to be your no-steps; one-steps; angle drills; and kicking on a line, sideline-to-sideline. It would be best to keep the reps on game day under three kicks apiece, in order to keep your leg fresh throughout the day. But, on practice days, you can do at least five kicks per drill and focus on the one that you really need extra help with.

Recap of Field Goal Drills

You don't have to do all of these: simply do the ones you feel you need help with the most. However, each of these drills are designed to improve your game just that a little bit extra.

A few of the drills to improve your accuracy might be:
- Angle drill
- Line drill
- Hit the upright from the sideline

The drills to work on height could be:
- Hit over the upright drill
- Clear the crossbar from five yards away
- Kick over a soccer goal from five yards away

Drills to work on ball contact could be:
- Barefoot drill
- Ball contact with a partner
- Ball contact with a ball on a stick
- Pole drills

Drills to work on swing path could be:
- Kicking down a line
- Hit the upright drill
- Draw a straight line from the ball to the target
- Foot preservation drill

While there are plenty of other drills that have been covered throughout this chapter, these will definitely serve the purpose of the category they come under. All of these drills will make you a better kicker. You simply need to: **TAKE ACTION!**

6
KICKOFF TECHNIQUE

It's just a longer approach with a hurdle at the end.

When doing a kickoff, really the only two differences are that it's a longer approach with more momentum and you're having a hurdle at the end if you choose to. A hurdle is very effective for getting all of your weight through the kick, as opposed to just skipping downfield. Both methods achieve the same effect, but a hurdle applies just a tad more explosion through the ball. Just because you're farther back, don't think that equals more power. It's about leveraging that additional distance back from the ball and transferring that momentum to get more force on the ball.

Also, the more speed you have does not mean more power and distance—quite the opposite. Typically, the farther back and faster you go, the more out of control you are and the more chances there are for an error. The harder you try to kick the football, the harder it is to kick. Trust the process and your swing and everything else will take care of itself.

Smooth is power, and power is smooth.

Find YOUR kickoff steps

Once I found my steps then I could consistently repeat the same kick time and time again. Finding your kickoff steps can take some time, and I would be lying if I said I never change my kickoff steps. In terms of finding your steps, there are a bunch of different ways that kicking coaches will teach it. The easiest way I found was to go from your natural instinct and work from there. So, in order to find your steps, the process is fairly simple:

Step #1 Put the kickoff tee on the ground, then step up to the plant spot and face where your starting position will be when you are ready to kick.

Step #2 Depending on your comfort regarding how you wish to start progressing towards the ball, you will either begin with your left or your right foot forward. For me, as a lefty, I would start with my right foot forward (since I jab with that on field goals): I'll take my first step with my right foot, then left, right, left, right, left, right (planting step), then kick. For me it's two-three-two for my step count. If I wanted to start with my left foot forward, I would go three-three-two. The first two-to-three steps are almost a walk. The second set of two-to-three steps are a medium pace jog. And then the final two-to-three steps are a faster-pace jog.

Step #3 Once you get to the place where you feel you would kick the ball, do a natural swing on where the ball would be. After that, go back to where your plant foot landed and go backward to find your steps.

So, from your mark, take normal walking steps across until you get to the kickoff tee, then take steps forward until you physically get to the tee. For example, if your mark is four steps to the side, you would physically take four steps in until you reach the same line as the kickoff tee; and if it's nine steps forward, physically take nine steps forward until you get back to the kickoff tee. Now, for added reassurance, do the drill two more times and take the average mark of the three reps. That will be your kickoff ready position.

Really the goal of this drill is to have you find your kickoff steps in a natural way, which will give you the most consistency possible. Do not stutter-step or take long strides at the end in order to reach your mark; start slow, pick up the pace gradually, and then the final two-to-three steps should be your energy-transfer steps. So, for me, doing this drill I would take a small jab step with my right foot (since I'm a lefty); my second step is my other walking step; my next three steps are a slower jog; then my final two steps (my energy-transfer steps) end at the plant spot, so I can adequately get up and through the football and finish ten yards upfield.

I'll take it if you're reading this part and just want someone to tell you some kickoff steps you can do on your own, try 3-3-2 (that's three walking steps, three jogging, and two at a faster-pace jog). Or 2-3-2 (this simply involving one less walking step). The main difference here is which foot is starting the momentum. With 3-3-2, your kicking leg will be the first step; while 2-3-2 will start with your plant foot, just like a field goal. Personally, I do 2-3-2 since I like feeling the same beginning rhythm as a field goal. But everyone is different, so do what makes you comfortable!

Tempo

Years ago I saw Dustin Hopkins practice his tempo before kickoffs—and it seems it works really well for him as he now plays in the NFL. ;) All he would do before every kickoff was clap his tempo out in order to catch the rhythm. After some time, the audience started to catch on to this and repeat it back to him: further solidifying his tempo. I'm not saying you have to clap for each kickoff, but having a routine down to an exact cadence can definitely help with confidence for your kickoffs. You want to go to a point when you can simply clap it out and it makes perfect sense and then you just have to do it. As mentioned earlier, you don't want to come into the kickoff at full speed. Control your progressive speed, and maintain composure on your technique, and the ball with start to fly as a result.

Controlled power

Since the kickoff can be three times farther back than a field goal, there are a lot more things that can happen to alter ball flight and consistency. That's why maintaining such a disciplined approach to the ball and not deviating from your line is so important. Often, kickers will run either to the ball the whole time and then curve back at the last step to their plant spot; or, they're going straight to their plant the entire time and then their last step goes in towards the ball and then back towards the plant, which is another reason why the ball either shanks or gets hooked heavily after contact.

Point your body, hips, and shoulders going straight towards your plant spot, especially on that last step, because that can do wonders for you if you maintain your alignment. You'll really have to fight for alignment on your last step, but again we want to keep our energy going straight; anything less than that can take away from the momentum you just worked so hard to get. Likewise, the main thing is that nice, tall body posture throughout contact: as this will give you more height on your kickoff.

The hurdle

This part can get fairly confusing, so try not to overthink it. The hurdle is the weight transfer at and after contact for your kickoffs. Essentially: when you come in to plant your kicking leg, kick through the ball, and as your kicking leg is in the air you transfer your weight to your kicking leg, to land on it and continue running downfield. A lot of kickers will really try to gear up, and almost look like they're about to fall after the hurdle. Again, there's nothing wrong with this, but you don't want to risk injury during a kickoff just because you hurdle with 110% effort. One other thing about this is to try and not hurdle off to the side away from your target zone. You want your transfer to go forward, as opposed to left or right. That's when you will know your weight distribution was on point. This is where drawing a straight line past the kickoff tee can help give you a visual of where to swing. Do your best to swing between eleven o'clock and twelve o'clock if you are a lefty, and one o'clock to twelve o'clock if you are a righty.

Help your team out

We all love a big kickoff, but that's all fun and games until the other team scores because you kicked it so low that they had plenty of time to figure out the route that they were running to. On the other side of the coin, a very high kick that doesn't go far also doesn't help much either. Most coaches want to do tons of pooch kicks. It's frustrating, because you're guaranteeing that they start from the 25, 30, or 35, if not way closer—because sometimes most teams don't even call a fair catch.

If you can't kick it out of the end zone every single time, to give your team the best chance for success it's heavily encouraged to do directional kicks if your coach doesn't already do so. That way, if you kick it to the 3-yard line in the very corner of the field, it's a heck of a lot harder for them to return the football since their opponents are on one side and they only have half the field to work with a large majority of the time (as opposed to kicking middle kicks, where they have both sides to decide from in terms of where they want to go). Choosing for them limits their ability to give a solid kickoff return.

80/20 lean

Earlier in this book we talked about lean out for field goals—how it should be about 60% of your body leaning out, with the other 40% being engaged at contact. Now, for kickoffs, that should be cranked up to about 80% leaning away from the ball, with the other 20% engaged and locked at contact. The reason for this is that, by getting so much more momentum and torque coming in from a five-to-ten-yard run-up, you want to be able to maximize the height and distance on your kickoffs. The fact you can hurdle after the kick helps you really get that needed momentum shift and transfer through the ball at the point of contact.

Onside kicks

For onside kicks, point the tee where you want the ball to go. Place the ball with a slight lean forward. From there, take three steps back and two to the side. You should now be hugging the line you kick off from. When you take your steps, you want to plant a little bit in front of the football and hit the top third of the ball, swinging down and through. Act like your kicking toes are a pool cue and you're hitting the ball on the white stripe into the corner pocket.

The goal is to make it bounce up quickly and land twelve yards away from the kicking line. The ball needs to travel ten yards in order for the onside to be a legal kick. Otherwise it will be a penalty for being too short of a kick. Twelve yards is good because it will go far enough for the kickoff return front line to now have to be placed in an awkward position to catch the ball. (It also gives some room for error: i.e. if the ball only travels ten yards then it is still a legal kick, whereas if the kicker was aiming for ten and it went eight, that's a penalty.) It will take some practice, but make sure you keep three things consistent: step past the ball; hit the top third of the ball; and swing down and through with that big bone of your foot.

RECAP OF KICKOFF TECHNIQUE

- A kickoff is just a longer field goal with a hurdle at the end.

- You can get away with a slightly higher aiming point on the ball with kickoffs, due to not being worried about the opposing team blocking the kick.

- Just because you're farther back doesn't mean you have to swing any harder. Keep it smooth, and just swing your leg.

- The calmer you can remain during your approach to the ball, the more consistent you will be.

7
KICKOFF DRILLS

Hurdle drill

For this drill, all you do is put a plastic hurdle (or some cones) directly in front of the kickoff tee and a little bit more towards the side where you plant. Place this about a yard up the field to promote proper hurdling. This gives you a visual cue as to how far you should be aiming to land after your kick. Don't think you have to try to hurdle two and a half yards upfield after your kick in order to get everything through the ball. One yard upfield is more than enough space for a hurdle to take place.

4 x 2 drill

This is a drill best done right before full-approach kickoffs, and it is best done in three sections: the run-through; swing on-air; and with a ball.

A run-through is very simple. First of all, take four normal walking steps backward and two to the side, and take your kicking foot, putting it out in front. From the ready position, take the first step with your plant foot. Your second step is with your drive foot, and then land into your plant spot. From there, swing and simply land and keep the momentum going down your approach line.

If you draw a straight line from your toe to the plant spot, extend that same line past your plant spot. This is the line that you want to stay on for this drill. The goal for the 4 x 2 run-through is to simply run to your plant spot and continue running downfield through your approach line.

The next progression is a 4 x 2 swing on-air. Here you are going to add a swing once you land on your plant foot, but you still do not have a ball in this progression. Simply start with your kicking foot forward in your ready position; take a step with your plant foot; then with your kicking foot; land on your plant; and swing up, hurdling through downfield and finishing ten yards up the field. This will get you ready for the next movement of the 4 x 2, in which you will add the ball.

After you did five reps of run-throughs, and five reps of swings on-air, next up is to add a ball and do about five reps of 4 x 2 with that.

Full-approach run-throughs and swings on-air

Just like the 4 x 2, we will then do the same run-through and swings without a ball, just from your normal kickoff starting point. It's the same thing with your swings on-air where you get to your plant spot: simply keep everything the same in your technique, just remove the ball from the equation.

After five reps of run-throughs and swings without a ball, get into your kickoffs. We recommend to keep it to ten kickoffs or less. The kickoff movement is very explosive, so make sure you are smart about how many reps you do.

Cone drill

This drill is great for directional kicks, in which we are trying to place the ball in a specific location. (If your coach wants to do sky kicks, this is also a great drill for this: giving you a visual marker as to where your target zone is.) Make sure to get four cones, each bright enough so that you can see them from your kickoff spot. Put these cones in a square, preferably in the corner of the field, between the numbers and the hash marks. Now place the first two cones on the 3-yard line and the other two cones two yards deep into the end zone. Make sure to give yourself a five-yard target (since plus or minus five yards is fine, yet plus or minus ten yards is asking for too much).

If you have a hard time kicking to the goal line, then put the cones where you know you can confidently hit the ball every single time, distance-wise. For example, if I'm kicking off in the forty and I know I can hit a fifty-five-yard kickoff often, I would then put my cones on the 8-yard line, and then the 3-yard line. If you aim all the way between the hash marks and the sidelines, you will miss the hash marks and the sidelines. However, if you give yourself a five-yard aiming point, you might miss off about three yards in either direction, which is substantially better than ten yards off. With these drills, you have to aim small because then you will miss small.

Rope drill

This drill will humble you. Take a piece of rope and attach it from your plant foot in a straight line all the way to the plant spot, with the rope straightening out in between your plant foot and the ball. The goal of this drill is to keep both feet on the side of the "road" away from the ball and to not cross over. It is designed to prevent kickers who tend to sway or snake into the ball from doing so. This will keep you disciplined and straighten your approach, and your consistency will thank you as a result.

Finish ten

This is a simple mental note to have after each kickoff. Since momentum is such a huge part of kicking, be sure after you hurdle to finish ten yards downfield. That will ensure you're getting every ounce of your weight through the kick. Think of this the same way as your skip-through after your kick. It's the cherry on top of your already great kickoff foundation. Not only does it help for momentum, but you also help your coverage team out by closing out the angles the other team has available for a return.

RECAP OF KICKOFF DRILLS

- Get used to practicing with cones and aiming points to give yourself a target.
- Use rope for your alignment. It helps with your energy transfer and momentum towards the plant spot, which leads to big kicks.
- Do the little things right and, when the time comes, you're prepared.

8
PUNTING TECHNIQUE

Catch

When catching a snap for a punt, it's very important to keep your arms out in front of you, ready to receive the snap. Don't let the ball be caught with your arms bent as it can and will affect your get-off time. The faster you can make your catch, set, and step portion of your punt, the lower chance you will have of getting a blocked punt. You will find that, by being efficient, you give yourself more time to focus on the things that are necessary, such as your hand positioning.

Punting is about eliminating as many variables as possible, and simply catching the ball with your hands out will eliminate a massive one. Be in an athletically ready position, with your arms by your side. When the ball is snapped, will keep your arms out in front of you to catch the ball. You are now ready for the next step of the punt, getting set. So let's get to it!

Set (hand positioning)

When holding a football, the easiest way to think about it is it to pretend like you're about to shake someone's hand, and then simply place the football in your hand. Your fingers can line up with a specific part of the ball; but the more things you give yourself to focus on, the harder it becomes to do. Putting a majority of your fingers under the side seam works great. This allows additional support if there is a little rain or wet conditions, plus it also gives you a little bit more control over the ball than holding the top of the ball. When you hold the football, make sure that the laces are pointing off to the side a little bit. This is because the seams on the football can mess up your punt, as it's not a flat surface.

We want to give ourselves every advantage we possibly can take; so, the second you catch the ball, rather than having the laces point straight up at twelve o'clock, rotate your wrist to let the ball open up the sweet spot for you. And simply swing your leg up, keeping your momentum going forward, and balance yourself to utilize your momentum.

Act like you're going to shake someone's hand, then place the ball in there comfortably

Rotate the ball slightly, so you can hit the panel and not the seam. Tilt it so that the ball is facing one o'clock for a lefty and eleven o'clock for a righty

Steps

Depending on your preference, you can either be a one-step punter, two-step punter, or a three-step punter. Just be careful about the more steps you take because it can affect your get-off time. Throughout college, I was a combination of a one-step and a two-step punter. At Blinn junior college, I worked very hard on being a one-step punter: where my left foot would be forward, I would take a small step into my plant and then punt. In the beginning it was tough, but after some time it actually became my preferred way for over two years. It was very repeatable and explosive. Eventually, when I transitioned to two steps for a punt, I would start with my right foot in front, step with my left foot, land with my right, then punt it. Essentially I was giving myself about a half step more distance, but it felt less rushed and therefore more repeatable. Some people like to start with their plant foot forward; they catch the ball and do a hop, step, and punt. With practice, it can be a great way to punt a football—as long as you manage the distance you're covering. If not, be careful: because this can get blocked, since you're taking more steps than a one-step punter. Whatever the case, do whatever is comfortable for you; but ideally you want to make your steps repeatable and consistent for yourself.

Every punt is straight

Just like field goals: depending on if we are on the hash or middle of the field, it can make us think subconsciously that we have to do something extra to the ball to make it get to that specific location. That's exactly what gets us into trouble when we start hunting directional punts. No matter where you are on the field, every punt is straight. You shouldn't be going forward with your body and trying to swing and aim to the right because you want to disguise the punt. The second the ball is in your hands you want your body to be going where you're going to punt; otherwise, you're teaching yourself bad habits. So, rather than trying to do some fancy SportsCenter "Top 10" punts—where you go left with your body but you kick it right somehow—keep everything consistent and repeatable. At the end of the day that's what our job is on the field: we want to set our teammates up for the best chance of success by putting the opponent deep with little or no return. The second you try to get fancy, and aim the punt, is when your technique tends to fall. Rather: catch the ball, go where you should go, and punt that way. Your leg swing, in tandem with your body, should be going towards your target.

Body position

Body position is critical for punting. It becomes very hard to punt a football when your chest drops down, limiting your leg swing. On the other hand, if you lean way back, your momentum goes behind you, limiting the distance your punt can get. That's why I like the phrase 'nose over toes'. This really means setting your body up in a position where your nose is a little bit in front of your toes, promoting forward momentum. Maintaining this positioning throughout the kick will really help you drive the ball up and out if everything else also stays consistent.

The drop

One of the most important things to make sure you have down every single time is your drop. How can you expect predictable results if the ball is in a different position on your foot every single time? For a left-footed punter, the nose should be pointing at one o'clock; and, for a right-footed punter, eleven o'clock. The reason for this is because 99% of punters have some sort of a swing across—where they don't swing completely straight up through the ball. In order to combat that, a slight lean helps eliminate all swipes. Depending on if you're punting into the wind or not, the nose should be tilted down. In a perfect world, we would keep the ball completely flat, with no tilt up or down; but, since there are wind conditions, you will need to cater the football to them. If there is a wind in your face or slightly across the field, a slight tilt of the ball downwards will be necessary to drive it through the wind. (Vice versa: if you want the ball to stay up in the air, and the nose to continue to spiral, keep the ball tilted up a little bit more.) Likewise, if there is a wind in your face, consider lowering the ball slightly more than normal in order to compensate for this.

Leg swing

Punting a football is a completely different beast to field goals and kickoffs, and therefore it takes a different mindset to do them. The optimal technique for a swing on a punt is to extend your leg up—keeping your hips under you, rather than letting them pop back at contact. This keeps you balanced and makes sure the ball explodes up off your foot first, rather than going out. It's better to have a forty-yard punt at a four-and-a-half-second hang time than a fifty-five-yard punt at a three-second hang time. Height trumps distance in punting because you don't want there to be a return at all.

You want to put your team in the best defensive position possible by pinning the opponent deep in their own territory. Master the technique and everything else will follow. Flexibility is king for all things kicking, but primarily for punting. Since it's such an explosive movement, you should be stretching your hips out daily for at least twenty minutes.

Eyes

The eyes are such an important part of a punt because they keep you from wanting to see how pretty your kick is. Sure, everyone wants to see the beautiful punt they just had; but it's more important to make sure that your mental checklist is ticked off first, and then you can check out the punt. There is power in being able to keep your eyes down after contact, which not many people realize. For starters, doing so keeps your body more in control. This is because, subconsciously, you want all of your other body mechanics to work in conjunction with the good kick—as opposed to throwing everything out there and hoping for the best after you make contact. Pat O'Donnell is an amazing punter to watch for a great example of how to keep your eyes down at contact.

Follow-through

A great tip I heard years ago for a proper follow-through was 'swing your right foot to your right ear if you're a righty, and vice versa if you're a lefty'. This way you can be sure that you're not leaving anything behind on the kick; plus you really allow your body to help you throughout the punt, rather than limiting yourself by chopping at the ball or punching at it. A nice follow-through and extension in punting is critical. Why do you think Ray Guy was so successful? He is one of the greatest punters of all-time and he could put his leg completely vertical in the air. For a guy that tall, that's a weapon.

Explosion

For a standard punt, we want our extension and momentum to be going through the target, as that is what will allow you to get all of your weight through the punt. The main thing is that you don't let your leg sweep across your body. That severely limits consistency and power. Do everything you can to keep your hips and shoulders going where you want them to go and simply stay on that line, keeping yourself efficient. The better you can explode your leg up and get your body square to the target and through, the better hang times you will see, as well as greater power on the ball.

Balance

The same thing that applies to field goals also stays true here. Be in an athletic stance, ready for the ball to be snapped. The worst thing you can do is to hang around almost entirely on the heels of your feet. It will be bad once that ball gets snapped and it either goes over your head, or the punt gets blocked because you're not ready to move. Be in a ready position. The second the ball is snapped, catch the ball with your arms extended out so you can save yourself some precious time on your get-off. You want everything you do to be working for you, not against you. Catching the snap with your arms super bent would be classified as against you. Swinging across your body is against you. Do what will help you be the best version of yourself.

Body position

Since punting is such a precise skill, it's very important to limit any hindrances to your technique. One example of a hindrance would be leaning back at contact. Leaning back removes momentum from the punt, which is limiting to the overall distance. If you find your punts are going high as opposed to far, it's very common that your body position at contact could be leaning back. Instead, keep your nose over your toes and your shoulders forward throughout the punt. At no point during the punting motion should your shoulders fall back behind your feet. Everything is constantly moving forward, no matter what. As stated earlier, be ready in an athletic position—with your knees slightly bent and shoulders forward—ready to rock the second you catch the ball.

RECAP OF PUNTING TECHNIQUE

- Leverage is everything in punting.
- Go forward with your energy, no bouncing or hopping. Catch with your arms straight and go straight.
- The more variables in your drop, the more variables will show up in your punting.
- Have an aiming point in your head for each punt, then bring everything to that.

9
PUNTING DRILLS

Cone drill

Very similar to the cone drill from the kickoff section, its punting counterpart follows the same core concept—that it's important to maintain a straight line in your punting approach. Many punters want to deviate from their line to try to "aim" the punt left or right. Nothing changes, except the direction your body is going. The leg swing does not change; the drop does not change: you're simply either going left or going right with your body. You still keep a flat drop, with a slight tilt in and rotation of the laces, to avoid hitting the seam on the ball. All things kicking or punting are straight lines. The second we try to curve or bend our kicks is the moment we lose control over our kicks. Understand that no matter where you are on the field is simply a straight line from where you are to where you want the ball to go.

Aussie punts

This is a fantastic option for punts from the opposite 40-yard line and in. (Depending on leg strength, this can either become closer or farther away.) Aussie punts are awesome for pinning your opponent inside of the ten, giving your return team a great chance of getting downfield to either catch the football or let it bounce in the same place so that your team can grab the ball with ease.Essentially, the ball rotates in an end-over-end fashion: giving you a much easier and repeatable target (rather than your standard spiral punt option, wherein the ball is dropped flat). There are a few ways to hold the ball for an Aussie punt. The first way is the over grip. For this grip, you hold the ball like you would a soda can. This hold is great for beginners who are just now learning Aussie-style punts. This hold gives you more control than other holds, and is the most-used option.

The second style of hold is the undergrip. You simply put your entire hand on the backside of the ball, typically in the middle of the ball. This gives you the most support and the greatest ability to move the positioning of the ball.

There are a few key things that separate an Aussie punt from a traditional punt. The first is of course the hand positioning. Next would be the angle of the ball at contact. Rather than having the ball perfectly flat (horizontal), the ball should be almost straight up and down (vertical). This gives you a bigger surface area and greater consistency as opposed to the flat drop. Aside from the hand positioning and angle of the ball, the contact will be your most important part. Instead of swinging your leg up like in a normal punt, with an Aussie-style punt you're swinging out to drive the ball forward. Since the punt is end-over-end, it will have a harder time cutting through the wind. Focus on getting through the ball in order to give yourself the best chance for great ball flight and bounce.

Normally, on a standard flat drop, our foot will come right up through the center of the football: creating a perfect nose-down spiral as it turns over. With an Aussie punt, since you're holding it more of an up-and-down position, really make sure you are not hitting the pointy part of the football. You are going to aim just a little bit below the center of the football while keeping your momentum going forward to achieve an end-over-end punt that should go high and between the 10-yard line and the goal line. By the time it lands, your team should either be able to catch it, or the ball will not bounce much—making it an easy recovery.

On top of swinging through the ball, you need to make sure your foot is flexed at contact so that it's hitting off a flat surface. If done properly, once the ball bounces, it should only bounce about five yards forward or backward but no more. A perfect Aussie punt will bounce straight up and stay about a yard in front or behind of where it bounced, giving your return team a great chance to pin the opposition deep in their territory. Chiefly, this punt is best for those situations where it's just a little too far to attempt a field goal and a little too close to try to do a full-field punt. Since it's harder to hit these farther, make sure to practice often: so that you have this in your tool belt for when the time arises in which you need to pin the other team deep in their territory. Because, typically, if the ball goes over their head, they're thinking it's going to be a touchback—and so it gives your team a super-easy chance to cover the punt.

Have a slight lean back so you don't hit the point at the top. The alternative is to hold the ball like a soda can, where your hand is on top of the ball

Drops from a kneeling position and contact

This drill is great for getting consistent with foot-to-ball contact. Simply start in a forward lunge position, with your kicking foot as the knee that is down. The non-kicking foot is going to have the knee at a ninety-degree angle. You will then hold the football as if you are about to punt it: tilting it no more than eleven o'clock or one o'clock, depending on which foot you kick with. (Righties are eleven and lefties are one.) Any more than that and you will have difficulty getting a spiral, since it has to fight the wind. Your best drop is going to be almost straight, with a slight tilt in towards your body. At that point, with a relaxed arm out in front of you, simply drop the ball as flat as you can straight down. This allows you to repeat the drop motion quickly without any variables. The perfect drop should bounce up; or even a little towards you, given the nose tilt in.

The next advancement of this drill is to place your non-kicking knee on the ground. From there you will then extend your kicking leg and foot out in front of you, fully flexed and extended. Then take the ball, maintaining a completely relaxed arm, and drop it a little bit more on the outside of your foot. (So if I'm a left-footed punter, I would not drop the ball directly on the center bone of my foot; I will drop it just a smidge to the left of the center, for an easier possibility of a spiral at contact.) If we drop it just off to the side of our big bone, the ball will, naturally, spiral off the foot.

This drill works on the foot-to-ball contact. For a lefty punter, the perfect drop here would be to let the ball gently leave your left hand. As the ball is falling to hit your foot, the drop should be perfectly flat. The ball should hit the middle of the big bone on your foot and roll off to the left. For a right-footed punter, the ball will then make contact, and roll to the right and forward a bit. (You've done this drill wrong if the ball goes across your body, or bounces back at you after contact.) While focusing on the proper part of your foot to make contact, make sure you're keeping your shoulders pulled back and your spine straight. We don't want to force bad habits in these drills. Just simply pay attention to the posture you're in after doing this for fifty reps.

Do this drill on a knee without your kicking leg forward, and then with your kicking leg forward, for fifty reps each. Repeat this drill daily as it doesn't take much time to get down.

Commit to the line

Since everything is a straight line, whether you're doing field goal kickoffs or punts, committing to the line is just as important now as it was when you first started reading this book. Don't allow the fact that you're now doing directional left punts affect anything about your steps or alignment. Oftentimes opposing teams have no idea if you're planning on punting left or right based on the way your body is facing. Every now and then you might run into a team that knows you're punting a specific direction; but, if you're good enough, it won't matter. Just like in the kickoff rope drill, take a piece of rope and put it in a straight line to the direction of your target.

Your goal is to stand on the side of that rope and do not cross that. Simply trust and commit to the line of your target; keep everything the exact same; and just make it happen. Sometimes, when we have to punt in the direction opposite to our kicking foot, it can mess us up mentally. But I promise you there is no difference in any part of the field you're punting to—it's all mental. The only thing that differs is the way the ball fades as it starts to turn over. Though, at the end of the day, a well-executed punt won't move that much to the left or the right after it's kicked. Stay disciplined and trust your technique; the rest will take care of itself.

Track drops

There are mixed thoughts on doing drops around a track. The common issue with track drops is that it develops the habit of playing catch with yourself rather than practicing proper drops. The point of track drops are to give you a straight line to go down with enough space to do the drill for some time. (As opposed to taking two small steps, dropping the ball, picking it up again, and repeating over and over, which leads to you hunching over each time to pick up the football.) Instead, work on the quality of each rep. After you take your step to drop the ball, pause. Your body should be in an athletic position with your kicking foot back, and your shoulders forward: ready to smash a football if it was a live rep. Every single rep you do should be at game speed minus the physical kicking motion. Don't develop bad habits just for the sake of getting reps in. It's better to do fifty game-speed, perfect-technique reps rather than doing a thousand bad reps.

Drop tables

This drill has a simple purpose: to keep the ball completely flat coming out of the hand. The less the ball moves from the hand to the foot, the better. This drill can be done by going to a flat table near you and taking your standard catch, set, steps—and, when you drop the ball on the table, the ball should maintain a consistent bounce. The ball should either bounce straight up or ever so slightly at an angle towards you.

Explosion drills

This drill has a helpful way of getting you to understand the concept of proper momentum flow through the ball. When doing this drill, do not use a ball, as it's strictly for proper hip drive and posture. Get on the sidelines and imagine a snap to you, then go through your catch set, steps, and swing. Now, instead of swinging your leg, you are simply going to drive your knee up into your chest and lift yourself up off the ground as high as you possibly can. This drill is supposed to work on height and hip drive as well as body posture throughout the punt. Maintaining a shoulders-forward stance, simply bring your kicking knee up: getting yourself off the ground as high as you can to utilize the momentum you put forth.

Punt pass

Oftentimes when you're with your buddy practicing your punt or kick, we tend to lose sight of our form and technique and it can cause setbacks for us in the future. This drill is really to just warm yourself up and get used to the swing of your leg as well as momentum. Get on opposite sides of the field, kicking from sideline to sideline. One punter will have their kicking foot on the line of the field. Simply take a 50%-speed catch, set, step, and swing with the ball—trying to keep as smooth of a technique as you can. Keep your shoulders forward, relax your guide arm (the arm holding the football), stay tall, swing your leg up through the ball, and walk one to two steps downfield to ensure a great punt.

Again, be very careful when you're practicing drills with your friends as you tend to get carried away in conversation and, before you know it, you're not practicing the right technique. Focus and dial-in on the rep at hand, then you can continue your conversation after the kick or punt.

One-step drill

For the one-step drill, put your kicking foot out in front of you in a balanced manner. (You don't want all of your weight on the heel of your foot, nor on the balls of your feet.) You want a flat foot anchored into the ground. From here, take a powerful plant step no more than a yard forward and drive up through the ball.

This drill works on your generation of power from your side step into the plant. The goal is to keep this under one yard because small steps generate more power than big steps. When we take big steps our balance goes out of whack and we end up leaning back: taking away potential explosiveness from the punt at contact.

We want to maintain a shoulders-forward mentality while keeping a nice relaxed arm and simply drive up through the football in a straight line. This drill is best done going sideline-to-sideline to give yourself a visual as to where the ball and your next step will go. If your kicking foot is on the line, you do not want your plant foot to land on the line as well. We don't want one leg crossing over the other one. By crossing over, we allow our leg swing to swipe at the ball, promoting inconsistency. We want to walk in a straight line, and the punting technique should be no different. Keep your energy going forward and trust your form. Have a consistent flat drop just to the side of the center of your kicking foot and you will be golden.

RECAP OF PUNTING DRILLS

- Punting is more muscle memory than field goals. There are a lot of things that can happen in two seconds—control the controllable.

- Your drop is your best friend: do your drop drills with good form.

- The more you can glide the ball down to your foot, the better

chance you will have of hitting great punts.
- More drops = Better punters.

10
PROPER NUTRITION

Plans for athlete nutrition always appear to be altering. It seems like any time you want to improve your diet, or someone else's, the standards change.

While this might be frustrating, I'm here to help provide a little bit of guidance on diet and nutrition.

In other words: if creating a diet plan is super-complicated, sticking to it becomes the problem. We will go over some basic guidelines, which will then improve your nutrition.

ATHLETE NUTRITION 101 – MACROS

Macronutrients, or macros for short, are the three most important food nutrients that your body needs. They consist of fats, carbs, and proteins. Without going into too much detail and boring you to death, just know that they all function well together.

Oftentimes, people heavily restrict themselves of one or more macro group and it impacts their day/week/month.

So it's safe to say we want a balanced diet consisting of a healthy portion of all three. And—when we are referring to athlete nutrition—eating good, high-quality food makes you a better athlete.

WHAT ARE CARBS, FATS, AND PROTEINS?

This might seem simple, but I didn't learn this until I was well into my sophomore year of college, so don't worry if you don't know either. Therefore, understanding this will improve your playing experience and better your quality of life.

Carbs

Good carbs (or carbohydrates) are:

- Pasta
- Bread
- Rice
- Beans
- Fruits
- Vegetables

Good carbs just means healthy sources of fuel for your body, so that it won't feel foggy or lazy.

Bad carbs are:
- Candy
- Cake
- Soda
- Dessert
- Pizza
- Chips

All carbs are going to be your faster energy sources. If you want a good, quick source of energy, carbs are your best bet.

Low-carb/"keto" diets are not recommended for football players and/or sports that require intensive exercise for hours at a time. Since being an athlete takes a toll on our energy sources, it's best to replenish your body with healthy carbohydrates.

So, it's best to stay away from low-carb diets.

Athletes that require short bursts of energy need to have carbs.

A great physique allows you to perform really well without feeling sluggish.

Food is fuel, give yourself some of the good stuff!

Fats

Fats are the brain-boosters, heart-helpers, and the way to feel full.

While often small, they are the most calorie-dense—so be careful! Great healthy fats are:

- Avocados
- Cheese
- Dark chocolate
- Whole eggs
- Fatty fish (salmon)
- Nuts
- Chia seeds
- Extra virgin olive oil

While good fats ARE good for you, too much of anything can be bad. As a result, we recommend using a food scale.

Fats are, in my opinion, the easiest to overeat from. I remember the first time I started to measure portions. I thought a cup of milk was literally a full cup. It turns out I was getting three times the number of calories than a normal serving.

Even better, when I started measuring chicken, I thought one whole raw breast you get from Walmart was eight ounces, and I wanted to eat sixteen ounces a day. I was eating well over thirty-two ounces of chicken in one sitting, or well over one hundred and fifty grams of protein.

Some bad fats are:

- Butter
- Margarine
- Beef or pork fat
- Shortening

Although butter is used often, this is precisely the reason why it is bad fat. Imagine taking two meals: one meal of chicken, broccoli, and almonds (totaling three hundred and fifty calories, with healthy amounts of proteins, carbs, and fats); and then you take another meal—the same serving of chicken, broccoli, and almonds—but you add three tablespoons of butter to the broccoli to make it taste better.

Just with that small addition, you have added three hundred calories: almost doubling the calorie content of the meal! The crazy thing is, you could barely tell that butter was added if no one had told you. As a result, you just got a heaping amount of fat added to your food without your even knowing. That's the danger of added fats. They tend to provide no nutritional value, but can spike our calorie levels for each meal.

While it can get confusing to know what foods to eat, just think of food as good or bad quality of nutrients. If I eat this will it make me feel energized and alert? Or slow and lazy?

If it makes you feel bad after you eat it, you know it's not the best to eat compared to a healthier option.

But who am I to stop you from eating what you like? Just please do it in moderation; it's your life.

To sum up: how you feel and function is in direct correlation to the daily choices you make—from food all the way to fitness.

A great rule of thumb is that, if it's advertised on television or in the middle of the grocery store, it may not be the best-quality nutrients that your body needs. The middle of the grocery store tends to have most of the junk food since that's where most shoppers naturally go when they first enter. So stick to the outmost parts of the grocery store to give your body the best fuel for everyday performance.

Proteins

I could write a two-hundred-page post on protein alone. It is my favorite nutrient, since it helps build and maintain those muscles. If you want to improve metabolism, performance in your sports or daily life, eat more protein.

Protein Examples:
- Chicken breast
- Turkey breast
- Egg whites
- Dried fish
- Shrimp
- Tuna
- Halibut
- Tilapia

A common theme here is that most proteins are meats. Most higher-quality proteins are lean sources of meat that are over 80% protein.

Lower-quality proteins:
- Red meat
- Dark meat
- Processed meats

The reason these are low-quality is that they are either high in fat, or not made with natural ingredients. (If you have ever seen hot dogs being made, you'll know what I mean.)

As a result, you typically want to match your body weight in grams of protein. (if I'm one hundred and eighty pounds, I need to eat one hundred and eighty grams of protein daily.)

For example, this could simply be two scoops of protein powder (sixty grams), eight ounces of chicken (seventy grams), four whole eggs (twenty-four grams), and two servings of cottage cheese (twenty-five grams) to get you to around one hundred and seventy-nine grams of protein.

Simply put: protein makes us stay strong during our performances; develop good habits so you can become a machine on the field!

It may seem harmless to grab that bag of chips; but, trust me, your future self will thank you if you substitute it for something of higher quality!

Eating healthy is not easy, and that's why a large majority of the world has bad health. Those who place priority on their health and fitness are the ones who feel better, stronger, and more mentally energized to get more done in the day. So it is safe to say that if you put high-quality food in your body, you will get higher-quality results.

Develop the habit of going for the apple instead of the cookies. Switch out the added sugar in candy for the natural sugar in fruits. You'll feel better and be more full for longer.

If eating healthy were easy, everyone would be doing it. But that's exactly the point! It's far better to invest in your health than in medical bills in the future because you let your eating habits get the best of you.

RECAP OF NUTRITION

- Food is fuel: give yourself the good stuff.
- Eat a balanced diet with a higher priority in protein to give yourself the fuel you need to perform at an elite level.
- What gets measured gets managed. I would highly recommend getting a food scale and tracking your calories through MyFitnessPal.
- Drink. More. Water.*

*On top of all of the tips throughout nutrition, water tends to be such an overlooked part of everyday life. Our bodies are made up of over 70% water. Therefore, we need to constantly check in with our hydration to ensure we're performing at a high level. Proper water consumption promotes brain activity, which maximizes physical activity, alongside dozens of other benefits. Do you ever notice how, if you go a few days without drinking water, you start to feel tired and sluggish? Almost as if you are just off today? A great place to be mindful about begins with water consumption! Starting now, aim to drink at least half your body weight in ounces of water. So, If I weigh one hundred and fifty pounds, I will aim to drink seventy five ounces of water. However, I drink my body weight in ounces since it is what I feel my body needs. It's best if you start with some type of standard that you can achieve daily. Fifty percent of something is better than 100% of nothing. It would be best if you start with at least 'drink half of your body weight in ounces of water' if you don't drink any water already. Eventually, you should make it a goal to drink your full body weight in ounces of water.

11
MINDSET

This part of the book looks at the proper mindset you'll need to be your best—not only in playing football, but in life. The purpose of this section is that it can function two ways. First, you can come back to this book at any time to reconfirm something you might be working through or a challenge that you're facing; and you can also use it to learn and grow: to help you continue to climb the mountain of confidence and success.

The other way this section helps you is through its addressing thoughts, quotes, or approaches you may be using to get better. That's what life is: living in your true form and not falling short of your potential. This section will help you find the best version of yourself, so you can succeed on and off the field.

WHAT TO THINK ABOUT WHILE KICKING

This might sound counterintuitive, but the less you think the better you do when you're kicking/punting. You should treat your practice as an opportunity to improve on one—maybe two—things, but not a ton of different areas. Realistically, we end up getting nothing done at the end of the session the more we complicate things.

When you practice your kicks, treat it like a game rep. You're working on improving a few small tweaks, but, when you're about to kick, clear your head and just go. Nod to your imaginary holder, visualize a cadence in your head, lock-in, and make it happen. If you have access to someone who can hold and even snap a football, that's even better. More often than not, it's just you and the field goal holder at practice. But that solo role is exactly the position we signed up for.

By the time you take your third step back to get in the ready position, your mind should already be completely clear of all thoughts and you're completely locked into the kick.

The old saying "think long, do it wrong" could not be more true for something as specific as kicking. The hours spent practicing should be more than enough time to handle any thoughts you might have about your technique.

By the time the game shows up, just have fun. You've already put in the work during the week, now it's time to enjoy the fruits of your labor. Have fun, enjoy the process, and trust your swing—you got this! Everything else will take care of itself if you work hard and stay disciplined in your kicking routine. We will establish a proper warm-up routine a little bit later in the book for the workout section.

When you step on the field to kick the ball, you should be confident that the hundreds of hours that led up to this moment have prepared you. Simply take a deep breath, trust your swing, and knock it through. You've trained for this, and you are more than prepared: now it's time to make it happen!

FIND YOUR ROUTINE

One of the things that throws kickers off from practice to games is an environment they aren't used to. "The crowd is noisy." "The other team has some quick guys who might block my kick." "The wind is unpredictable today" and about a hundred other things that race through kickers and punters heads during a game can get overwhelming. Even if you are nervous during the game, one of the biggest thing I have noticed in the highest performing athletes in any sport Is their routine. Try googling a pro kicker or punter you really like and watch their mannerisms before they kick the ball. They might lick their fingers, shrug their shoulders, twist their hips to face their target, tap their kicking cleat into the ground. Whatever it is that they like to do, they have made it unique to them. And what's most important is that gets THEM centered within themselves so they are focused and ready to go for the kick.

So if you watch kick number one compared to kick number seven hundred and twenty two that they do, It looks completely identical. No matter how far back they are on the field, what the weather conditions are, what the crowd is saying, they are staying true to THEIR routine. That helps them stay calm even if they are nervous. They know that once they go through their whole set routine, they are prepared and ready to go. The rest will happen as it should. They just trust their swing and make it happen.

I suggest you do the same. Make sure to make your routine repeatable, and yours. Everyone has a routine that is perfect for them and makes them relaxed. You just have to practice enough times to see what you do or don't like. What works for me may not work for you and vice versa. So take some time to do some practice kicks around the field or at your house, try out a bunch of different set routines that will help you stay focused. That way when the pressure is on and you are called out to kick a huge game winner, you do your routine like you have a thousand times, and just like clockwork, you make the kick with ease. Pro tip: when you take your normal walking steps back, you should be lining your kicking foot up with the target, visualize the ball hitting a small and specific target you pick beyond the uprights (aim small miss small) take a deep breath in through your nose and out through your mouth. Take your side steps ninety degrees from where you are (every kick is straight, side steps less or more than ninety degrees will throw off consistency) When you get to your set position, you can take a look at your target once again and visualize hitting it, take one more deep breath through your nose, and out through your mouth.

If you want to add or subtract anything, be my guest, that's just what a vast majority of high performing kickers do so take what you want from it. After you do what feels comfortable, look back at your holder give a nod indicating you are ready to go and make it happen. When you practice by yourself, get in the habit of nodding to your imaginary holder to simulate a live rep. Take it a step further and picture your holder physically there along with the snap to his hands. That prepares you better for the real thing. And this goes for punt and kickoff as well. Find what centers you, breathe and go!

MINDSET FOR PRACTICE VS GAMES

As stated earlier, practice is more of a fine-tuning moment, wherein you're simply putting the pieces together that are in line with your natural swing. The point of practice is to get all of the ugly kicks out of the way and to make yourself 1% better. When practicing, this is not the time to kick a hundred footballs. It is a thousand times better to kick forty or fifty footballs with excellent technique and a clear intention as to what you're trying to do for each rep.

Please don't kick just to kick; each rep should be focused on developing something technique-wise, which will strengthen to consistency muscle. Do not waste any reps; learn something from each and every one. End the practice with the understanding that you got better today. While practice is meant to work on specific things to make you a better kicker, every single kick should be treated as a game rep.

CLEAR YOUR MIND

Kicking is over 70% mental, so you can imagine it's very easy for your thoughts to get in the way of your performance. With that being the case, we have to learn how to control our minds, and let them help us rather than hurt us. The easiest way to let your mind work for you is by being present in the moment. When you are present, you don't let your negative thoughts get in the way of you doing well.

You have to fully accept what your reality is so that you can perform at your highest level. Being present takes some time to get really good at, but there is an amazing video by a man named Eckhart Tolle that perfectly describes how to become present in the moment. Go on to YouTube and type in "How do we break the habit of excessive thinking?" It will lead you directly to the video, in which he perfectly sums up what he describes as the "in-between thoughts" (aka "being present").

Learn how to extend the in-between thoughts, and be more aware of that. You will get rid of the bad, compounding thoughts and simply become one with what is here and now. When I first heard about this it seemed pretty humorous; but, after the first day, I could see its potential. Soon after learning the power of being present, I started having my greatest performances on the field.

GO 1/1

When we kick, whether we made or missed the last one, we tend to hang on to that longer than we need. All such thinking is doing is making our next kick/punt harder. Especially when doing field goals, punts, or kickoffs, the only kick to focus on is the one you're doing. We set these audacious goals on what we want to accomplish for the season; "I want to go 18/21, or make 85% of my kicks." Great, but how can you make that happen?

Rather than thinking about having to make 85% of your kicks, why not just go 1/1? Break it down into a task that you're more than capable of doing. If all you did was focus only on your current kick, you would have a substantially easier time focusing and accomplishing the goal. All you have to do is lock into just this one kick. Then, once you make it, wipe that clean from your head; now it's on to the next one. Don't constantly think about what is to come, just know deep within what it feels like to make the kick, visualize your success, then move on to the next one.

BREATHE TO FOCUS ON THE NOW

If you're having trouble figuring out how to clear your mind and be in the now, your breath is an amazing tool for this. Simply take five very deep breaths and pay attention to the rising and falling of your stomach as you inhale and exhale. Oftentimes our nerves can run out of control right before we step onto the field for a kick. Next time you feel nervous/overwhelmed, use your breathing to send yourself back into the present moment, utilizing it to calm yourself. This will put you in a state where you're fully relaxed and present in the moment at hand. It sounds cheesy, but it really locks you into the current moment. What do you have to lose? Your negative thinking doesn't do anything for you. So let it go and enjoy what is around you. Utilize your five senses more. You have them, so why not enjoy them?

HAND-ON-BELLY BREATHING

If you have trouble focusing on your breathing, put your hand on your stomach, and pay attention to how it rises and falls from each breath in through your nose and out through your mouth. As mentioned earlier, feeling is believing so let's make sure we give ourselves an easy way to focus on the breath to calm ourselves down.

LONG-EXHALE BREATHS

To add to putting your hand on your stomach, slow down your exhaling breath to make it at least ten seconds. So a great way to get yourself centered again is to put your hand on your stomach, take a deep inhale breath for five seconds, and then exhale that breath for ten seconds. Repeat this for five reps. Should you feel like you are still needing additional clarity, continue until you reach the desired relaxation.

If you can get away from your thoughts and learn how to simply accept what is in this moment, you take away the anxiety and nervousness.

What is there to be nervous about? You cannot control what is to come or what has been; you can only control this moment in front of you.

Learn to lock in just like Adam Vinatieri and you will see your consistency skyrocket. Pat McAfee has spoken about how Vinatieri locks in during game-time, and it is both extremely humorous and very informative. Type in "Pat McAfee on why Adam Vinatieri is great" on YouTube. There is a distinct focus an elite-level kicker has when they take the field. That feeling is hard to describe without feeling it for yourself. Locking in happens when the audience drowns out; you don't hear anything; and it's just you and the ball. The moment passes by so fast you don't remember anything.

That's why throughout this book we talk about getting uncomfortable as often as you can, so that when the moment comes or your team needs you most, it's a walk in the park. Lock in and let's make it happen!

"AIM SMALL, MISS SMALL"

This term is such a useful tool for kicking. Imagine a very small target zone, and line up to take the kick. When you go to kick the ball, you are now setting yourself up for a really good chance of making it; because, simply by aiming at an extremely small target, if you don't hit the target then you're more than likely to miss just a little bit to the left or to the right of it. However, if we aim between the posts, it's more than likely that we will miss left and right of the post. As the saying goes, "Aim small, miss small". So, simply by aiming at a big target such as between the uprights, it becomes easier to miss, since you're aiming for it—so what did you expect to happen?

In contrast, by picking out a target much farther and higher away than the uprights, you are setting your sights on something past the objective in front of you. That way, if for some reason you don't happen to hit the object way off in the distance, you will still make the kick. So, for example: if there is a flagpole directly behind the uprights, don't aim for the flagpole—aim instead for the brass knob or whatever object that sits on the top. The point is, don't just aim for a target: aim for a specific object within that object. So if the word "TITAN STADIUM" is what you're aiming for, then, within that, the top-right corner of the "N" in titan would be a great aiming point. After aiming, take a quick second to visualize hitting the target. Simply have faith in your technique and form, then make it happen.

- Find an aiming point higher and farther than the uprights.
- Aim for a smaller target within the target.
- Visualize yourself hitting the target.
- Trust your swing and make it happen.

> *"I fear not the man who has practiced 10,000 kicks once, but I fear the man who has practiced one kick 10,000 times."*
> *– Bruce Lee*

There's something to be said about consistency. It's not about going out there and kicking and punting one hundred times just to say you put in the work. It's about practicing one specific kick a hundred times to know you put in the work. The one who stays diligent in his practices and does not deviate from his plan is the one who will succeed in the end. The other kicker, who just wants to go out and kick as many as possible until his leg gets tired and then go home, is not going to be making real progress three months from now. Meanwhile, the kicker who consistently does drill work, stretches, and applies a lot of the other principles we will teach you in this book, will not only become better in three months but will continue to improve month after month by maintaining a disciplined, consistent effort.

> *"Give me six hours to chop down a tree and I will*

spend the first four sharpening the ax."
- Abe Lincoln

This quote serves two purposes. The first relates to strengthening and developing the tools necessary to accomplish the task. Rather than kicking for two hours straight, spend an hour and a half stretching, warming up, and doing drill work. Then spend the other thirty minutes kicking. Doing small things correctly, day after day, creates success.

The other dimension of the quote has to do with discipline. You have to have the discipline necessary to continue chopping down the tree. A lot of us just want to go straight out and start kicking right away. But doing something tedious involves putting in the work over and over again until it's done.

BE A STUDENT OF THE GAME

If there's an overarching theme that EVERY professional kicker/punter has, it's being a student of the game. Not only are they kicking/punting, they will then review the film from their session, make notes, review their notes, and ask What thing, if any, could I do better here?

Sometimes you hit a great ball and there's nothing you can improve on. That's perfectly fine! However, if there's a consistent issue with the way the ball flight is looking, or you're just having trouble with this one specific thing, take a step back and film it once or twice, go frame by frame and see what looks weird, then work to fix it!

For example, a few sessions ago, for the life of me, I couldn't hit a kick without getting an X-ball. After filming a few kicks, I found that my consistent issue was that I was hitting around the ball and my toe was coming up. So I went back, made a focus to lean out to the side more so that my body got more leverage and I could make sure my foot was hitting the correct location of the ball. Sure enough, by doing that one little thing, the rest of the session went great.

The main point here is: don't ever stop looking for ways to learn more about your technique. A lot of kickers/punters let their ego get in the way of them and their improvement. That's why a ton of them start to fall off later in high school or in college—because they think they're better than the other guy but they don't put in the work to prove it. Only the kicker/punters who go in each day with the mindset that they are great at what they do, yet who are always looking for that thing that can give them that 1% improvement, are the ones who find real success.

I've seen so many kicker/punters let their ego get the best of them. Stay humble, work hard in everything you do, and never stop learning.

And, by the way, this tip doesn't just stop at sports. You should always be a student in any field you go into in life. When you have a burning curiosity for something and you actively want to find out the answer, the sky is the limit.

ASK YOURSELF THE HARD QUESTIONS

The really cool thing about personal development is it can be never-ending if you choose for it to be. So many people who succeed in life attribute a lot of their success to the difficulty of the questions they ask themselves. They find that, when you do this, your brain has to find the answer; even if it's not a fun question to answer, it can be just what you need to hear.

There's a massive difference between, "Did I do good today?" versus, "Are the actions I put in today getting me closer to that person I made a promise to be by this time next year?" Or, "Is this the type of thing I need to be doing in order to achieve the level of success I am capable of reaching?"

Now, when you put yourself in an awkward position, you have to find an answer from somewhere. These hard questions are going to make you much better, and much faster, since there's no other answer than the right one.

After reading this section, the right thing to do is to upgrade the questions you ask yourself. You owe it to yourself to search for better, and to be better in the process.

DOING THE LITTLE THINGS

How do you eat an elephant? One bite at a time.

How did professional kickers get to become professionals? By doing the drills, working out, stretching, filming, and reviewing their kicks. No professional kicker is an overnight success; they spend five, ten, fifteen years working for the opportunity to play on the big stage.

Let's take two kickers: kicker A, and kicker B. Let's say they both kick fifty footballs a day for five days a week for an entire year. Kicker A simply goes out there, stretches for five to ten minutes, kicks all fifty footballs, goes home, and then repeats this the next day. Kicker B goes out there, does an extensive warm-up and stretching routine, does the proper drill work and kicks twenty-five footballs with great form and technique. On top of that, he films his entire session to reference and review later. After an entire year, who do you think will be the better Kicker? You get five gold stars if you chose kicker B.

When you break it down, you'll find that the biggest difference between the average kicker/punter and the pro is that the pro just does the basics better. They are more disciplined than everyone else. They actually do the stretches in the morning and night; they workout even when they don't want to. Their nutrition is in check, they make sure to work on punt drops, no-steps, contact drills, etc. They do all the seemingly boring stuff because they KNOW it will only make them better. So ask yourself, What would a pro do in this situation right now? Then just do that.

You see, it's really about putting effective, concentrated effort into the things that will truly help you. Sure, doing a full rep can teach you—but what about all the other aspects of kicking that many people neglect? Watch a professional kicker/punter and I promise you they are working on the drill work and stretching extensively day in and day out. The little things are what it's all about.

To add another tool to your belt, on top of filming the kicks use OnForm—this app will help you with your film reviews. What's great about the app is it gives you a frame-by-frame analysis of your swing.

When you want to go further than that, you can do a side-by-side comparison of two kicks/punts. Whether it's you on both videos, or another kicker/punter, you can see what the differences are and what that means to you.

One example could be me kicking a field goal. I then take a video of Justin Tucker and compare what are our similarities and what does he do that I could work on? These types of comparisons will give you the upper hand, especially if you find a role model kicker/punter and in every kicking/punting session you compare your technique to theirs.

Another really cool thing you can do is overlap two videos. This is also huge because you can sync up two different kicks and see areas for improvement. For example, if I had a fantastic kicking session a few weeks ago but today I was struggling more than usual, I can overlap the two videos to get a much better idea of my tendencies. Oftentimes, you're not doing anything wildly different. You could just be dropping your chest down more than you normally do. As a result, the height you normally get isn't there and the trajectory suffers.

Something else you can do is to overlap your role model kicker/punter, to see what they do and what you can improve on. Technique-wise, Joey Slye, Jason Myers, and Matt Prater all have really efficient swings. They don't leave any body weight behind the ball. They are great about getting every bit of their momentum through the ball, with little-to-no wasted movements.

By comparing your form to theirs, you are subconsciously trying to replicate some of their biggest strengths, improving your game in the process.

This applies not only to form and technique, but to their overall habits. Learn what they do outside of kicking: whether it's workouts, daily practices, their mindsets, etc. Write down what you like and start applying it. Success leaves clues and it's up to you to pick up the crumbs.

Exponentially growing has never been easier. The tools and resources are out there for you to be the best kicker/punter you can be. You just have to utilize them.

PRACTICING ON YOUR OWN

Throughout your practices, it's very important to treat each rep as a game rep. The point of practice is to improve one or two technical adjustments. But during your practice, right before you kick the football, clear your mind and treat each kick or punt as if you were in a live game; mentally visualizing the snap, cadence calls, and crowd noise. Try to get as much of a realistic scenario as you can for each kick. If you really wanted to practice kicking through distractions, put on some headphones, YouTube "distracting noises" turn the volume up and try to kick through them. You'll know you are able to focus really well when those noises do not even faze you at all.

DON'T OVERTHINK IT, JUST KEEP IT SIMPLE

There is a common expression, "Keep it simple, stupid", or KISS. It is a really great way of saying "Don't overthink it". Especially in kicking/punting, the more you think, the harder it gets. The best kicking sessions you'll have are when you're barely thinking, in which you're feeling your natural swing, and trusting your technique. Going out there with a few things you want to work on are important. But the most important thing is to keep your kicking crazy simple. Have an intention for each kick as to what you would like to do technique-wise, and just make it happen. If you have trouble staying tall on your kicks, stay taller. If the ball is curving on your kicks, swing more at one o'clock or eleven depending on the foot you kick with (one for a lefty, eleven for a righty). When you think long, you do it wrong. Keep it crazy simple. Relax, enjoy your sessions, and you'll do a ton better!

HOW TO GET OUT OF A SLUMP

What's important to notice is that slumps are normal. That way, you shouldn't become too down on yourself because you're having one. In the grand scheme of things, you have to remember that this too shall pass. Keep a smile on your face and keep on moving.

From time to time, if you really want to get perspective on how small the slump you're going through matters, look up at the sky and remember that we are a speck of dust in the universe and nothing that's happening for you (not to you) will matter in ten years.

It definitely doesn't matter right now because tough times are the moments for you to grow mentally. Use it as an opportunity to flex your toughness muscle.

While there's no way to fully prevent a slump from happening, there are some guiding principles to adopt in order to minimize the effect of one.

If you find yourself going through a tough time in the future and need a mental reset, use the acronym BE HERE:

- **B**e aware that this too shall pass
- **E**xercise to get your mind off of what you're going through
- **H**ave a moment to meditate
- **E**nter thoughts in your journal
- **R**ead to open up your mind and creativity
- **E**njoy the moment here and now

FINDING MEANING IN SLUMPS

As the cliched saying goes, "Everything happens for a reason". I bet you're a bit like me: where you make a big deal out of something small and insignificant. Oftentimes we hold on to those missed kicks, the hot streak of no sales, the consistent losses, and other forms of slumps longer than we should. Rather than viewing it as something that's happening to you, realize that it's happening for you.

Life is such a beautiful teacher, if we allow it to be. We can choose to be upset and sad about every little thing that happens in our life, or we can be optimistic and understand that all of these little things need to happen in order to make us stronger for today, tomorrow, and next year. Think about the future you, and how strong he or she will be if you continue to grow in your mentality and mindset. Granted, it may not be extremely easy to find the positive light in all that we are going through—but that's exactly the point. Life never gets any easier; we just get better. If you allow yourself to see the opportunity in the moment you are given, great things are bound to happen.

> *"Don't wish it was easier; wish you were better.*
> *Don't wish for fewer problems,*
> *wish for more skills. Don't wish for*
> *fewer challenges, wish for more wisdom"*
> *-Jim Rohn*

I love the quote that says, "It's what you're going through, it's not where you're staying." Again, you can choose to dwell on all the things that are wrong in your life, or you can choose to understand that things will get better, and you're going to come out on the other side a better stronger, happier, healthier human being.

Life is a choice and we have the option every single day of our lives to choose to do the right thing. Some take that opportunity and some don't, but that's their life. You have to know you control what you can control; no one else is going to hold your hand through this stuff your entire life. The earlier you can understand that these moments are only temporary and things will get better, you'll be better off because of it.

LET IT GO TO MOVE FORWARD

In the belief system of Taoism, one of the core beliefs is in the power of letting go. Oftentimes when we really want something that's all we focus on, and it seems as if the desired result is just out of reach. Almost magically, the second we let go of that thought or the desired result, it tends to find a way back into our lives faster than it ever could have done if all we did was focus on that one thing. That goes with anything in life: health (a certain body fat or body weight); financial status (a certain amount of money to be reached); or relationship-wise (actively looking for a girlfriend). It was almost humorous how this exact belief worked in my own life. The second I was able to separate myself from the desire to want a girlfriend, I met my life partner Polina almost two weeks after that. She mentioned the same thing in a conversation we had—the moment she stopped looking for the thing that she wanted, it came into her life gracefully and without resistance.

Because what you'll come to find is that, when you let go, you allow yourself the freedom to move forward in the direction you want. So try this now: think about the thing that you really want so much that it's almost stressing you out; take a deep breath and realize "It will come if it is right for me. I simply have to stay disciplined and faithful"; but don't obsess over what it is that you want.

A lot of field goal kicking and punting can relate back to golf. They are extremely similar in a lot of ways. The biggest similarity is the mental aspect. You could be the strongest golfer in the universe but if your brain can't focus, if you have a hard time forgetting about the past, you will have a very short career in golf. You've got to be able to put your mistakes behind you and focus on the rep at hand. There is an amazing movie with Will Smith and Matt Damon called The Legend of Bagger Vance. It's about a golfer who is struggling and he meets someone one day who ends up being his caddy and mentor. Without spoiling too much, as the movie goes on you see the mentality of the main character, Rannulph Junuh (Matt Damon), start to shift with the help of Bagger Vance (Will Smith) and his golf becomes progressively better.

It's an amazing movie that is relatable to kicking in many ways. One specific part of the movie is when Bagger Vance helps Junuh "find the field". The video clip to search is "Bagger Vance – Finding the Field" on YouTube.

By conquering your mind, you open up so many more doors to your potential—not only in football, but in life.

Visualization

A really important thing to do right before you kick or punt is to visualize a perfect rep in your mind. How does it feel when the ball comes off your foot perfectly; cutting through the wind, not being affected by it at all? How does a crowd sound when you make the kick? How are you celebrating with your teammates after you pin the opponents deep in their territory after a beautiful punt?

First, you have to see it in your mind. You need to feel the emotions as you go through the rep in your head. The more senses you can involve in your visualization, the more realistic it becomes. Then, the more likely it is to become a reality. Because adding attention to detail subconsciously creates the environment for us to actually make it a reality. For example, rather than just visualizing a ball going through the uprights, visualize the kick in full color from both a third-person perspective (as if someone were watching you kick the football) and a first-person perspective (where you are physically kicking the perfect rep). Not only that, but as you are on the sidelines you should be visualizing the ball passing through the uprights and the referees holding their arms up to signal that it's a good kick. Or visualizing your recovery team downing the ball on the 1-yard line and running over to celebrate with you. There is a massive power in being able to imagine and visualize a rep with all of your senses.

> *"Those who think they can and those who think they can't are both usually right"*
> *– Confucius*

A study done back in 1996 showed the power of visualization. A basketball team was split into three groups for a month. The first group was told to physically practice shooting free throws every single day of the month. The second group was told not to even touch a basketball, but to visualize the ball going in the hoop every day for thirty days. The third group was told not to do anything. After one full month, the first group, who physically shot a basketball, had a 24% improvement in performance; the second group, who strictly visualized, showed a 23% improvement; and the group who did nothing showed no improvement.

That's wild! The group who shot each and every day did only a small percentage better than the group who didn't even touch a basketball! Yet, they seemed to have worked much, much harder. That is the true power of visualization.

Now take those numbers and pair them with a group that does both the physical-shooting free throws and visualizes the free throws. It's fair to say that there will be a dramatic increase in performance if you utilize both physically and mentally practicing the reps. The more variety you add to your visualization, the better results you will have. Again, by imagining it in your mind in full detail, you make the chance of it actually happening much more realistic.

POSITIVE THOUGHTS

We all know the power of positive thinking, but you don't typically find the information online for kickers and punters. Thinking is just as important here, as it is the thing we do most often in life. We have over 60,000 thoughts per day and a vast majority of them are negative thoughts. Now, imagine if all we did was change 10% of our negative thoughts into positive ones—you think you would notice a change? OF COURSE! They do not even have to be dramatic, over-the-top positive thoughts; by simply being aware of our internal chatter, we can change the dynamics and direction of what we do on any given day.

If you think you hit low field goals, you will. But if you think "I just hit a low field goal right there, but it's okay because I know that just means I need to follow through a little bit more and drive up with my leg", you have just changed your mental chatter. Likewise, if you think you always miss left, you will. But if you think "I'm only missing left because my hips are slightly back at contact. I just need to square up with my target a little more at contact and I will be able to make those kicks right down the middle every single time", you can see how—just by being aware of your thoughts, knowing what it takes to fix them, and then making that your new go-to reality—you will start to see incredible improvements in your consistency.

The hardest part is simply noticing when we're being negative in our thinking. That is why meditation and the constant practice of being present is so valuable. It takes us out of that draining, negative-energy headspace and puts us into a more productive mindset. So try it next time you go to kick/punt or when you're around in general. Be aware of your thoughts and convert them from a more negative style into a positive, productive, and learning-focused one.

"I can't" becomes "I will".

"I don't know" becomes "I will find out".

"That's not possible" becomes "It's probable".

"Let's hope" becomes "Let's do it".

"Don't mess up" becomes "I've got this".

FEEL AND EMBRACE IT

As mentioned earlier, when you are visualizing don't simply think about the rep being performed. Feel the way the ball hits your foot; your perfect swing path and technique; listen to the crowd cheering; imagine your excitement as the ball goes through the uprights; think about the celebration with your teammates. The more realistic you make the kick, the better chance you have of making it. Eventually, you will become adept to the point that you can harness that feeling of celebration. It's powerful to know that at any moment on the sideline you can put yourself into a state of relaxation; one of confidence, knowing that you are the man for the job.

PROTECT YOUR BRAND IMAGE

The power of social media is much stronger than a lot of people know. Within seconds of posting, you can reach hundreds, thousands, or millions of people. You can change your life with one post on social media, for good or bad. So with that being said, you should treat your social media as a résumé.

If you feel like you want to create a personal page where you post about your own life, do that, and then have a separate social media specifically for your kicking/punting material. That way you don't clog up your feed with too much of one or the other intertwining. In terms of branding, it's a good practice to post as if your grandma is going to be looking at your posts. Once you run it through that filter in your head, the decision on whether or not you should post becomes a lot more clear.

Another filter to throw in there is to imagine the school/job of your dream coming across that photo and either being really impressed, or thinking that that just helped them make the decision as to why they should not pursue you as a player/prospect. Whether you're in kindergarten, elementary school, middle school, high school, college, the pros, or any field in any industry, protect your brand and image and be proud of the things that you post.

The right person could come across your feed at any moment and change your entire life, so be conscious about what you put out into the world.

RECAP OF MINDSET

- Mindset is everything to a kicker. Never stop learning.
- Read books!
- Breathe more when you feel overwhelmed.

- You've got this. You may not be ready, but you are more than capable.

12
MASTER YOUR MORNINGS

YOUR MORNING ROUTINE

You don't really hear from many people about routines prior to your getting on the field. You typically just hear about warm-up routines and stretches in order to prepare you for the game or for the practice. The morning routine is almost just as critical as your field warm-up. There are a million ways to get your day started in a positive direction. We will do our best to highlight some of the most beneficial techniques to set yourself up for success.

Wake up early

If you find yourself always in a rush and not having enough time in the day, you might consider waking up earlier than you normally do. To demonstrate the reasoning behind this, let's take two people: person A and person B. Person A wakes up every single day at seven; person B wakes up every single day at six. After one full month, person B would have had thirty more hours to use on themselves. That is more than an entire day's worth of time extra for them to do what they feel is necessary. Let's turn that one hour into two hours. You now have sixty hours, or over two and a half days, of additional time per month that you have given yourself by getting up just a little bit earlier. Over a full year, that's seven hundred and thirty hours, or an entire month! You get an entire month out of the year by just waking up two hours earlier each day! Talk about utilizing your twenty-four hours.

How can I wake up earlier? you might ask. I'm already exhausted when I get up at seven. Well, there are a couple of answers to this, but the majority of the time you could just be telling yourself you're tired and therefore you think you're tired. Don't let excuses get in the way of the success you were meant to have. Sometimes, sure, you might not be getting enough sleep. Science shows that seven hours is recommended, but six is more than plenty. Personally, I get on average about five hours of sleep and I have no complaints. When you know what it is you're waking up early for and you plan your day out ahead of time, waking up earlier is a lot easier. Because, once you wake up, you already have a preset number of things you are trying to accomplish and you simply knock them off the list one by one. By the time seven rolls around you will have completed multiple tasks and therefore gotten a head start on the day.

The essentials of a morning routine

There are some core components of a successful and healthy morning routine. The necessary basics of which are:

- An alarm clock.
- A sixteen-ounce glass of water.
- Workout clothes.
- A book.
- Journal, piece of paper and a pen.

Each one of these materials are going to be necessary for your morning routine. They all play into each other efficiently. The next question you might be asking yourself is, What kind of morning routine would require all of these items?

Preparation for the next morning and when you wake up

The night before your morning routine begins, it helps to set your future self up for success. Fill up a glass of water and put it next to the bed. Prepare your journal or piece of paper by putting tomorrow's date on it, along with goals and tasks on what you want to achieve for tomorrow.

Next, set your alarm thirty minutes for earlier than you normally sleep, and then the next night you can bump it back another thirty minutes. Just make sure to compensate for your sleep by going to bed a little bit earlier, thus compensating for your earlier wake-up.

While I can't force you to wake up at five a.m., you will find yourself in a great mood having accomplished some of your biggest tasks early in the morning.

Another secret to success is accomplishing your biggest task first-thing when you wake up. You'll find you have more momentum if you can take on the biggest challenges first, and that you get a snowball effect going into your other tasks.

Put your alarm **far out of reach** from your bed so that you have to wake up, and must physically get out of bed to turn the alarm off.

If you struggle with the snooze button and find yourself in the "snooze paradox"—wherein you might snooze up to five times before actually getting out of bed—download the app Alarmy. It does a great job: making you enter math equations in order to turn the alarm off! (Not only that, some of its alarms are very obnoxious, which is something I need since I'm a heavy sleeper.)

Really what it means when you continue to press snooze is either: you're not motivated enough to attack your goals and dreams; you like being abruptly woken up, multiple times; or you must really like the sound of your alarm. There are plenty of other reasons as to why you're not getting up early, but those tend to be excuses.

I promise you: if your alarm is placed across the room away from the bed, and you immediately then go into the bathroom and brush your teeth, wash your face and drink some water, you'll get your energy level up from a two out of ten to a six.

Your workout clothes can be put in the room you brush your teeth in so you can get changed immediately. Through all of these small preparations, you make your morning routine a lot more productive.

One last helpful trick I like to do to wake myself up is to brew some hot tea. By the time you get some hot tea or coffee in your system, you should be at around seven out of ten.

If you don't have access to hot tea or coffee, that's perfectly okay. Just do ten jumping jacks to get the blood flowing.

The morning routine

After years of working on developing a morning routine, Hal Elrod designed a routine that would not only help you physically but mentally and spiritually too.

The components are:

- **S**ilence (Quiet Time).
- **A**ffirmations.
- **V**isualization.
- **E**xercise.
- **R**eading.
- **S**cribing (Journaling).

Below is a template you can use and refer to whenever you want to make your morning routine. Silence is the first step.

1. SILENCE

The first step of the morning routine is silence. This is the time to take time for yourself. I am a man of God and spend the first ten minutes of my morning praying and just talking about the good and the bad of what's going on in my life. The point for me is I am actively building a better relationship with the Lord, holy one, universe, etc.—whatever you feel comfortable referencing. A critical way to get in touch with and further develop in my religion is through communication. Other times I'll just sit and express gratitude to God and listen to what comes back. If you find that you don't want to pray, you can meditate, or just have your quiet time. Personally I like to do the Wim Hof Method meditations after prayer, since they are different in their purposes. For me, prayer sets intention and gratitude for what I have; and then Wim Hof meditation (or meditation in general) helps me go deep, to get closer to myself and my spirit.

What I would recommend is to experiment with different forms of meditation and then stick to one that you like for a period of time. This is not intended to be a black-and-white, "You must do this" instruction. Do whatever you like, but make it impactful.

I've found that the Wim Hof Method puts me into a deep space of relaxation; one I am normally not able to go through traditional meditation.

What is the Wim Hof Method?

Now more than ever people tend to be looking for an answer as to how relax and calm themselves. Meditation is not a new practice, but many people have added it into their routines as a way to stay calm. The Wim Hof Method has emerged as a style of meditation that provides many health benefits.

Some of the most significant health benefits include:

- Stress reduction.
- Faster recovery from physical exertion.
- Better sleep.
- Improved sports performance.
- Enhanced creativity.
- Greater focus and mental clarity.

These and a few others are the reason I have become a full supporter of this style of meditation.

DISCLAIMER: Please do not attempt this method while driving, in a body of water, or in any other potentially dangerous situations. There might be a possibility of fainting, so please make sure you are in a safe and quiet environment when doing the method.

The Wim Hof Method is made up of three core components:

- Breathwork
- Cold therapy
- Fitness

Wim Hof Breathwork

The Wim Hof Method starts by getting comfortable. Sit on a chair, couch, lie on the ground, or however you can fully relax. (Personally, I like to lay on the ground since I am most calm in that position.)

- Take a FULL Breath in, and LET GO. Don't breathe out all of the air. (The goal is to take in as much oxygen as possible, without forcing an out-breath.)

- Then, on the thirtieth breath, you exhale, AND HOLD, without any air in the lungs.
- Without air in the lungs, you will be able to retain a breath for much longer.
- The second you feel like you want to breathe again, take a full deep breath in, and hold for fifteen seconds.

That was one round.

You will repeat this for two to three more rounds. (I have found that three rounds are more than enough to get myself to relax in a deep, alkaline state.) If you feel any tingling or lightheadedness, that is perfectly okay: it is a natural response to the breathwork. You may find that you are in a deeper state of relaxation than you have ever been before in your life.

Wim Hof's philosophy

Wim Hof talks about how, by taking deeper breaths, we are able to pump more oxygen, and therefore blood, into the body. Therefore, we increase our mental state, lower anxiety, and can relax more. Not only has this been proven, but his 100,000+ website members are advocates of this method.

Now, by no means am I telling you that you have to do it. BUT, studies have shown significant health benefits to the body following this type of practice.

But, again, whatever method works best for you works for me.

If you ever type the word "relax" into Google it won't be long before you find the word "meditation" somewhere in the search results. The practice of meditation is really just a way to calm your mind and relax your body. There are many ways to do meditation, but they all really revolve around one core concept—that meditation is really just a form of deep breathing. One of the more simple ways to do meditation is called the "box breathing" (also "square breathing") method. This is easiest understood when seen drawn out, but I will first quickly explain it. You start by taking a deep breath in for four seconds; you hold it for four seconds; you exhale for four seconds; and you hold the out-breath for four seconds. Then you repeat again.

Box Breathing

```
                  Breathe in
              ┌── 4 Seconds ──→──┐
              │                   │
              │          4 Seconds│
       Hold   ↑                   ↓   Hold
              │   4 Seconds       │
              │                   ↓
              └──←── 4 Seconds ───┘
                  Breathe Out
```

It's a great and easy way to meditate, especially if you're having a hard time relaxing. The one I personally like to use is just to focus on my belly rising and falling as I breathe in and out. I can even take it a step further and visualize the air flowing into my lungs as I breathe in and out. You can also use a form of mantra, whereby you repeat "I breathe in peace, and exhale stress". (There are many other mantras out there, and that is just one example.)

If meditating just by yourself feels a little difficult, I sympathize. That's why I like to do guided meditation through apps or videos. My favorite meditation apps are Waking Up (my all-time favorite) Headspace, Insight Timer, and Ten Percent Happier. They all have different styles and levels for users, but Waking Up and Headspace would be my recommendations if you are just getting started. Insight Timer has the greatest variety, and Ten Percent Happier has the most detailed courses that I've seen.

Personally, I love Waking Up because the instruction is so detailed and different from most other apps, which simply tell you to focus on your breathing. Trust me: there are a lot of ways to go deeper into a state of calm other than just that.

From all of these methods, below is a simple way to meditate and control your breathing:

1. Sit upright (either on a chair, couch, or the floor).

2. Get in a relaxed position.

3. Place your hands on your knees.

4. Take a deep breath in for four seconds; hold for four seconds; exhale for four seconds; and hold for four seconds. Then repeat. Do this for at least five minutes.

5. If you find your mind wandering, focus on the breath, or use a mantra of sorts:

6. "I breathe in peace, I breathe out love".

Meditation is one of the best ways to calm your nerves and become present in the current moment.

I would say you should try all of the aforementioned apps, to get an understanding of what you like; though try not to just bounce from one to the next without really committing to each first. I would say to at least give each individual one a try for a week, at which point you can decide if you like it or not. After you've committed to each app listed above (and/or any others you wish to try out), then you can figure out which are worth keeping/getting rid of. The point is to use the apps that you feel you can get the most value out of. Try them out for yourself and see!

Give yourself that gift, and practice your meditation!

2. AFFIRMATIONS

Affirmations are a great way to rewire your brain and start changing your internal dialogue.

Are your thoughts constantly telling you that you're not good enough? Affirmations are a great way to break through that barrier.

Write down some of your biggest weaknesses, and areas in which you really want to improve. These are the types of things a successful person would tell themselves in order to achieve their dreams.

For example, if you struggle with weight loss, you might tell yourself, "I make healthy decisions each day; not because they are easy, but because they are the right thing to do."

Or, if you have a hard time with your field goals, you could say, "Each field goal I kick is another opportunity to improve and get better from. I am learning from each kick I take as it will make me a better kicker for years to come. My future self will thank me because I am improving each day, in every way."

When you change your internal dialogue, you can change your external life.

Give yourself the gift of positive self-talk.

3. VISUALIZATION

This was covered earlier, but it's so important that it needs to be said again.

Visualization and affirmations are great when they're done one after another.

The reason behind this is because affirmations are things you tell yourself which you know are going to happen.

Visualizations are about seeing it happen.

Simply close your eyes, and think about how you feel, and look at that moment you wish to achieve.

For example, if you want to lose thirty pounds by the end of the year, imagine yourself looking in the mirror: with a big smile on your face, a great physique, the feeling of having worked so hard to achieve this goal, and the ability to say you did it.

Or think of making a game-winning kick against your rival in the big championship game: your walk out there with 100% confidence that you are going to make this big kick; then you imagine your perfect technique; then you kick the ball with such precision—it is such a great kick, it's the best kick you could do, and it clears the uprights by thirty yards; then you run down the field to celebrate and your team picks you up and you're now being held aloft by your teammates. Everyone's got huge smiles on their faces and you're completely happy in that moment.

Now take a step back and internalize that feeling. Make that visualization real, because it will be even more achievable the more detail you give it.

Again, put yourself in the moment you want to achieve, and use all of your senses to be in that moment. How does everything feel around you? What does it smell like? What do you see? What do you hear? The more senses and detail you have in your visualization, the more likely it is to happen.

4. EXERCISE

Good-quality exercise is one of the best ways to get your brain moving. While most of the other morning routines we've talked about are about ten minutes, exercise is one of the only ones that would be best done for twenty minutes or more.

While there is nothing specific to be prescribed—as everyone's health conditions vary—a good, heart-pumping workout to really get your body going would be best. Personally, a good weightlifting session with a barbell and resistance bands is more than enough. I found one of the best ways to increase my strength and explosiveness was to lift moderate-to-heavy weights and use resistance bands at the same time. The weight was heavy enough to where I could still be explosive on the way up, and control the weight on the way down. Resistance bands are great anywhere, anytime. They are portable, and excellent for adding resistance you can't get with traditional weights.

Keep going

When we get tired during a workout, oftentimes we've only reached a small percentage of our full capacity. Jocko Willink, Navy SEAL commander and author of the bestselling book Extreme Ownership has a beautiful way of putting it. He says,

"That pain you're facing is just short-term discomfort. It will end. When it comes down to it, it really just takes a second to take a step back and look at the situation. Ask yourself, 'Am I actually unable to go anymore or do I just not feel like it?' Almost every time, we can keep going and we need to trick our brain into thinking we can take one more step because it's not that you're tired, we just don't want to be uncomfortable. So when you start to think you can't go any further, realize your brain is telling you you're tired, but you still have plenty left in the tank. Just touch the weights, get in a ready stance, and set yourself up for the next rep. We just need to get ourselves in the position to get going and our muscle memory will take over to help us finish the task. It's a feedback loop to help you keep going."

When you're feeling tired during your workout, don't think about how tired you are—think about how strong you're getting by continuing to go when the average person would have stopped five minutes ago. If you want to be extraordinary, you have to put in extraordinary effort. Our brain will always look for reasons to stop and you have to look for reasons to keep going. There's nothing I or anyone can say to help you push past your next barrier; it really has to come from within, and you have to push yourself when no one else is looking. That's what makes a champion.

5. READING

As Jim Kwik says, "Leaders are readers". Some books are an entire author's life lessons in three hundred pages. Authors spend years writing a book: take Napoleon Hill's Think and Grow Rich. It took him twenty years to conduct all of those interviews. It's incredible to know you can obtain two entire decades of knowledge in just a few short hours. It's a no-brainer that everyone should read more.

By reading even ten minutes a day for three hundred and sixty-five days means that you will most likely read ten books or more during that time. And if you read over ten books in a year, it's safe to say that you will develop tremendously.

If, like me, you're a slow reader, look into speed reading by Tim Ferriss. It's a great way to double your reading speed, and therefore double your growth.

You can read whatever genre interests you, but personal development books might be your best bet for developing a healthy morning routine.

6. SCRIBING

Scribing (or Journaling) is essentially writing down your thoughts, experiences, feelings, and ultimate goals on paper. Many studies have linked journaling to increased creativity, better focus, more gratitude, and a reduction in anxiety and depression. For a more in depth analysis of this study, check out the references.

Simply grab the journal you wish to write in, try not to think so much, and just let the thoughts in your brain come on to the paper. It's also cool to look back on this and see where your state of mind was at any given point. Not only is scribing great for writing your thoughts down, but it is also a good practice in terms of daily gratitude, goal writing, and things that make you excited.

I did this when I was kicking footballs back in college. I would write my thoughts and feelings on paper after every practice so I could go back later and review them. If I had a bad day, I wrote about it! The same goes for a good day. You should get everything you can on paper and check back on it later down the road. This is a super fun way to see how far you have come, and what you went through to get to where you are now. It will be sure to ignite some internal emotions as you read your journals from days, weeks, months, and years ago.

Jim Rohn, an American entrepreneur, said "A great way to review your journal is at the end of each day, week, month, and year. By carving out time at the end of the day, week, month, and year, you can relive what happened, whether good or bad, and you can see what led you to where you are now. Take the necessary time out of the day/weekend to go over the journal entries."

It's inspiring to see the progress you've made. But, if something isn't working out the way you intended, the book of your life is far from over. The book is still being written, so what will you do to change it? Do you want your life to be one that inspires others? Or do you want it to be an average one that tells the story of someone who fell short of their potential? YOU have the capacity and ability to change the sails where you are going—begin now! There will never be a perfect time to change your life; you just have to get the momentum going and figure out the rest along the way.

The most important thing to remember is to **have fun** and document everything. You won't remember how you felt when you ran your fastest mile time. But if you wrote it down right after you did, you would definitely be able to relive more of it than if you didn't record anything at all.

Last thing on scribing/journaling

Make sure you're not just putting one sentence down a day, i.e. "I did good." Really go deep into your day so you can extract the full experience, and get emotionally involved with the moments you experienced. There will be some days where it will be tougher than others to block out ten minutes to one whole hour of writing. But trust me: it is one of the most rewarding things you can give yourself. Also, wether you're having the best day of your life, or one of the worst ones ever, put it down in a journal. Some of the biggest breakthroughs I've ever had can be attributed to journaling with the full intention of getting everything down on paper. So before that little voice in your head gains too much power over you, encouraging procrastination—the longer we take to do something, the harder it becomes to achieve it—take action: grab some paper that's laying around the house, and something to write with. You'll be happy you did it.

AFTER THE WHOLE ROUTINE IS DONE

After the routine is finished and you feel ready to tackle the day, the last thing is to throw yourself in a cold shower! It's best to do this following the routine, as you want to feel like you've earned it.

How to do a cold shower

Turn the water to the coldest it can get, and really, really, focus on taking full deep breaths. This will warm up your body and take your mind away from the fact that it might be cold. Just remember: in the shower, you are in control! If the water is unbearable and you feel like you need to build up to it, start with the water on warm, then, for the last thirty seconds, turn it to cold and take deep breaths. You've got this! You're going to feel much better once you go through the discomfort.

The benefits of a cold shower include:

Reduced stress levels. Regularly taking cold showers imposes a small amount of stress on your body, which leads to a process called hardening. This means that your nervous system gradually gets used to handling moderate levels of stress. The hardening process helps you to keep a cool head the next time you find yourself in a stressful situation.

A higher level of alertness. Cold showers wake your body up, inducing a higher state of alertness. The cold also stimulates you to take deeper breaths, decreasing the level of carbon dioxide throughout the body, helping you concentrate. Cold showers thus keep you ready and focused throughout the day.

More robust immune response. Scientific studies have found that taking a cold shower increases the number of white blood cells in your body. These blood cells protect your body against diseases. Researchers believe that this process is related to an increased metabolic rate, which stimulates the immune response.

Increased willpower. It takes a strong mind to endure the cold for extended periods of time. By incorporating cold showers into your daily routine, you are strengthening your willpower, which benefits many aspects of (your) daily life.

Weight loss. Research has shown that cold showers (and exposure to cold in general), in addition to increasing metabolic rate directly, stimulate the generation of brown fat. Brown fat is a specific type of fat tissue that in turn generates energy by burning calories. Cold showers, then, are an effective tool for people who are looking to lose a few pounds.

While you should take cold showers after your meditation, some people take them right before they meditate, it is up to you. However, the shower serves as the cherry on top of your experience. If this might seem overwhelming at first, try it with hot water and for the final 30 seconds, switch to cold and see how that makes you feel. Remember, you are in control!

HOW DOES A MORNING ROUTINE HELP YOU?

A morning routine will set your entire day up for success if done correctly. No matter what the day brings, if you can conquer the morning, it's a great day.

For the people who struggle with nagging thoughts in their head, self-doubt, or a lack of confidence—or, for the person who wants more out of life—a morning routine will be your main place to start.

Even if you take ten minutes to focus on yourself in the morning, that's a lot better than the person who didn't get out of bed.

Who should do a morning routine?

Anybody anywhere should have their own version of a productive and healthy morning routine.

The morning routine above really works for the person who wants more out of their life, and to live the life they were born to live.

If you or someone you know has trouble finding direction in their life, feels like nothing is working, or just doesn't know where to go, developing a healthy morning routine should be the foundation.

Developing a morning routine for school

School was never a passion of mine. But, during my time there, I valued the importance of time management, especially as a student-athlete. Therefore, my mornings were some of the most important times for me. (My routine worked for me and is what I got used to given our schedules. You do not have to follow this one, I am just providing an example of what I started doing to get the most out of the twenty-four hours we all have)

My ideal morning routine for college football would be:

3:55 Wake up

4:00–4:10 Brush teeth, put water on face, put on workout clothes, make the bed, drink a glass of water

4:10–4:20 Meditation

4:20–4:35 Affirmations/visualization

4:35–4:45 Read

4:45–4:55 Scribe/journal

5:00–6:00 Workout (either with a team or on my own)

6:00–6:30 Recovery/stretch

6:30–7:30 Eat

7:30–8:30 Study

9:00–12 Class

See how much can be accomplished in the morning before nine o'clock. For some people, they're just getting up at eight thirty for the nine o'clock class. At this point, I've already been up for four and a half hours and have already gotten a ton of stuff done.

Now, this is what I did for the last year at school, and loved it. I simply went to bed around nine to ten p.m., and got after it in the morning.

You can create the life you want to create by making it a focus each and every morning!

How to stick to a morning routine

There are definitely going to be days when you don't feel like you want to get out of bed. Believe me, I've been there where the bed whispers your name in such a sweet, comforting way. And all you want to do is curl up and "snooze" for another five minutes. And then those five minutes turn into one hour, which turns into two hours. Then, before you know it, you haven't even gotten out of bed yet and you have to leave for class/work in twenty minutes.

Therefore, the hardest part is getting out of bed. Once you get moving and wake up, the morning routine goes a lot smoother. That's why I recommend putting the alarm across the room and using an app like Alarmy.

Eventually, getting up early won't be a problem anymore.

The best way I have found to stay dedicated to a routine is to grab a calendar and cross off each day when you have accomplished your morning routine. (This is something Jerry Seinfeld did for years when writing jokes.) Go to Youtube and search for, "Seinfeld calendar."

For example, if I go five days in a row accomplishing my morning routine, I will have crossed out each individual day. As you'll notice, you have a streak going, and now you don't want to break the streak. Your one and only goal is to keep the streak going!

As you've just seen, there are many benefits to a morning routine. But at the end of the day, the most important thing is that it gets you to the place you deserve to be. I know you want to be the best version of yourself; just get out of your own way to make it happen!

RECAP OF MASTERING YOUR MORNINGS

- Wake up earlier.
- Practice some form of the SAVERS daily.
- *Anything* is better than nothing.
- Win the morning so you can win the day.

13
PROFESSIONAL KICKER/PUNTER Q&A

In this section, we reached out to current and former professional kickers and punters and asked all of them the same questions. This achieves a few things: helping us understand how they think, showing what they do to keep themselves performing at a high level, and giving an understanding of the mindset necessary to be elite. Enjoy!

GIORGIO TAVECCHIO

— 80.8% conversion in the NFL; has kicked for the 49ers, Packers, Lions, Raiders, Falcons, and Titans. Has also played in the XFL and Italian Football League.

Instagram: @tavecchiogiorgio

Twitter: @Tavecchio40

WHAT GOT YOU STARTED IN KICKING?

A casual invitation from a friend and a delicious team barbecue.

WHEN DID YOU KNOW YOU HAD A FUTURE IN KICKING?

When I started hitting touchbacks and 50-yard field goals my senior year of high school and I started falling in love with the art of kicking.

WHAT ARE THE MOST HELPFUL THINGS YOU'VE DONE TO PROGRESS YOUR KICKING SKILLS?

I found the no-step and the one-step drill really useful. I also think my core training routine has been instrumental in helping me become more balanced, more explosive, and more flexible.

What does your perfect day look like?

My perfect day begins with a great cup of coffee, followed by training on the field, then spending time with family/friends, and enjoying great food.

Describe your pre-kick routine and mindset for games . . .

My pre-kick routine involves focusing on my breath and keeping my awareness of executing my technique as best as possible. My mindset for games is to be as present in the moment as possible and to be as calm as possible throughout the entire day.

What's the one thing you would tell your younger self if you were just getting started?

I would tell my younger self to soak up and enjoy every second of this wild ride.

What's the most helpful thing you do when you feel overwhelmed or stressed?

I rely on diaphragmatic breathing to keep myself calm and centered. I also rely on my Faith to keep a positive and grateful attitude throughout the good, the bad, and the ugly.

Who has made the biggest impact in your kicking career?

I've had the good fortune of having many wonderful mentors over the years. In particular, I'd like to highlight David Akers, Michael Husted, and Nick Novak.

FAVORITE BREAKFAST OR MEAL FOR A GAME?

Pasta!!!!!!

Favorite workout to develop leg strength and speed for kicking?

I really like single-leg lunges, plyometric box jumps, and core exercises.

WHAT'S YOUR FAVORITE STRETCH? (IT CAN BE STATIC OR DYNAMIC.)

My favorite stretch is the T-Spine stretch, which helps to loosen up the lower back.

YOUR FAVORITE FIELD GOAL MOMENT?

Just seeing the ball go through the uprights is cathartic to me.

WHO DO YOU LOOK UP TO?

I've had great role models in my life, starting with my mom and dad, who have been instrumental in teaching me respect, consideration, and service.

CADEN NOVIKOFF

— First-team all-American at TVCC, going 89% on field goals his sophomore year. He then transferred to University of Houston and is currently an NFL Free Agent.

INSTAGRAM: @CADENNOVIKOFF

TWITTER: @BLASTIKOFF

WHAT GOT YOU STARTED IN KICKING?

I got started in kicking because I was a soccer player and I could kick the ball farther than most other kids.

WHEN DID YOU KNOW YOU HAD A FUTURE IN KICKING?

After my sophomore year starting on varsity, I knew I had the ability to take kicking to the next level.

WHAT ARE THE MOST HELPFUL THINGS YOU'VE DONE TO PROGRESS YOUR KICKING SKILLS?

The most helpful things I have done to progress my kicking skills are: filming my kicking sessions and watching them, studying some of the pros' film, and making sure I focus on something when I go out to kick.

WHAT DOES YOUR PERFECT DAY LOOK LIKE?

A perfect day for me would be to have a great kicking session with fresh legs and then hitting a solid leg workout and relaxing for the rest of the day.

DESCRIBE YOUR PRE-KICK ROUTINE AND MINDSET FOR GAMES . . .

My pre-kick routine would be to hit a couple balls into the net and to focus on my swing thoughts. And my mindset for games always is to be confident in my kicking.

WHAT'S THE ONE THING YOU WOULD TELL YOUR YOUNGER SELF IF YOU WERE JUST GETTING STARTED?

I would tell myself to just be patient and trust the process and keep working hard.

WHAT'S THE MOST HELPFUL THING YOU DO WHEN YOU FEEL OVERWHELMED OR STRESSED?

When I feel stressed I always try to take my mind off of what is causing the stress.

WHO HAS MADE THE BIGGEST IMPACT IN YOUR KICKING CAREER?

I have two people that have made a big impact on my kicking career and that would be: Sergio Castillo and Nick Gatto.

FAVORITE BREAKFAST OR MEAL FOR A GAME?

My favorite pregame meal was chicken and pasta.

FAVORITE WORKOUT TO DEVELOP LEG STRENGTH AND SPEED FOR KICKING?

My favorite workout is running stadiums because it works speed, strength, and explosion.

WHAT'S YOUR FAVORITE STRETCH? (IT CAN BE STATIC OR DYNAMIC.)

My favorite stretch would be pigeon pose right now, but I also like the World's Greatest Stretch as well.

WHAT'S YOUR FAVORITE FIELD GOAL MOMENT?

My favorite field goal moment would be when I hit a 45-yard field goal against Texas Tech to put our first points on the scoreboard.

WHO DO YOU LOOK UP TO?

I look up to a few different people but the main one is Sergio Castillo.

NICK NOVAK

— San Diego/LA Chargers 2010s (2010-2019) All-Decade Team.

Ranks sixth on All-Time Chargers Scoring List (503 points), UFL Record 54-yard field goal.

INSTAGRAM: @8NICKNOVAK

TWITTER: @8NICKNOVAK

WHAT GOT YOU STARTED IN KICKING?

I was a pretty good soccer player that took all the free kicks. My science teacher/head coach noticed the kicks and convinced me to come out and hit a few balls with the football team during practice. From that day forward the game changed my life. My mom had one stipulation for Coach V: kicking only! So the deal was made and all was good.

WHAT ARE THE MOST HELPFUL THINGS YOU'VE DONE TO PROGRESS YOUR KICKING SKILLS?

Practice often and learn to do the drills the right way. The no-step progresses to the one-step, then full. Each one has a purpose that builds onto the next, and doing them right and often made me really become a consistent ball striker.

WHAT'S THE ONE THING YOU WOULD TELL YOUR YOUNGER SELF IF YOU WERE JUST GETTING STARTED?

I would tell my younger self to buckle up: it's going to be a wild ride. Love the Lord, outwork everyone, be a leader, have fun, and never quit. Be prepared to play this game deep into your thirties. Be a blessing to as many people as possible. Be humble and grateful.

WHO HAS MADE THE BIGGEST IMPACT IN YOUR KICKING CAREER?

Coaches have made a huge impact in my career: from my dad as my first coach to the hundreds of coaches along the way. Most importantly family has always been there to lift me up when times got tough, and been there to celebrate all the victories. Through it all, my family has always treated me the same and been the most consistent. I'm blessed to be able to say that.

What's your favorite stretch? (It can be static or dynamic.)

Dynamic stretching before training, and static after.

Favorite workout to develop leg strength and speed for kicking?

Lunges, squats, cleans, deadlifts, and reverse hypers weighted. I love the weight room so these are just a few of my favorite exercises. Sprint work is my favorite leg speed exercise.

Favorite breakfast or meal for a game?

I would always eat oatmeal and eggs for early games and steak and potatoes for late games. I drink a lot of water throughout the game day starting the night before.

What's the most helpful thing you do when you feel overwhelmed or stressed?

Whenever I felt overwhelmed or anxious I prayed and did breathwork and it always seemed to relax my mind and body and direct those feelings to focus.

Your favorite field goal moment?

There were many moments that were memorable; to just say one was my favorite wouldn't give the rest the credit they deserve. What I loved the most is when the field goal team contributed to a winning performance. There was nothing like being in a winning locker room celebrating that victory together. Football is the greatest team game in the world and every kick that crossed the line of scrimmage had a chance because of the ten great teammates helping me do my job.

WHO DO YOU LOOK UP TO?

I look up to Jesus the most. This entire experience as a football player would have never been possible without his grace and belief in me. I always wanted to try and represent his faith in me through my play and in my day-to-day life.

SERGIO CASTILLO

— Was a 2019 CFL All-Star (91.1% on 41-45 attempts) and CFL West All-Star. Has played for the Atlanta Falcons, New York Jets, Winnipeg Blue Bombers, Ottawa Redblacks, Hamilton Tiger-Cats, BC Lions, and other CFL and XFL teams.

INSTAGRAM: @ELSERG41
TWITTER: @ELCASTIDELSUR

WHAT GOT YOU STARTED IN KICKING?

In my freshman year, my soccer coach came up to me and said "I've seen you kick a football and the football team is looking for a kicker. The guy that they had as a starter, they kicked him out because of misbehavior issues." And you know my soccer coach, Tamez, he's the one who open the doors for me to kick at La Joya High back in 2007.

WHAT DOES YOUR PERFECT DAY LOOK LIKE?

I wake up every day in the morning at 4:49 a.m. and then I get a nice little juicy lift at 5:30 in the morning. I'll kick right after that if the wind is not too crazy here in Amarillo, Texas. A good day for us is a good fifteen-to-sixteen mile per hour wind. It gets a little too crazy sometimes so I try not to kick on those days, and then go golf after. If it's cold then it's really not worth going: just because the wind/cold kills the vibe.

FAVORITE BREAKFAST OR MEAL FOR A GAME?

It's a big meat lover's omelet: you've got sausage, ham, and bacon in there with jalapenos. On the side I'll have two big pancakes with a warm cup of coffee.

FAVORITE WORKOUT TO DEVELOP LEG STRENGTH AND SPEED FOR KICKING?

I'm really big on Olympic lifting ever since college. Those are hang cleans, power cleans, snatches, and then obviously your squats. More than anything now I've been doing a lot of single-leg work ever since I tore my ACL back in 2017. I've also been doing a lot of track workouts. Those are very short distances, but they work on being as explosive as possible within a short time frame.

MICHAEL GEORGETTI

— NFL Free Agent combo kicker/punter. Six years' arena/indoor experience.

INSTAGRAM: @MGK30

TWITTER: @MGK30

WHAT GOT YOU STARTED IN KICKING?

At first, I really did not have any interest in football. I played soccer my whole life. When I was in high school, I got cut from soccer and sarcastically the coach said "If anyone gets cut, go kick or something, lord knows they need help." I did just that and fast forward about twelve years or so, now I'm entering my seventh professional season in the arena football scene with some amazing outdoor opportunities/workouts along the way!

WHEN DID YOU KNOW YOU HAD A FUTURE IN KICKING?

I was self-taught. I didn't have a coach until college really. So when I was in college and I started working with a coach privately. It was then that I noticed how much fun I was really having. And I knew I didn't want to stop after college. But really it was my first kicking coach. He groomed me to be a professional as well as play professional and I did just that.

What are the most helpful things you've done to progress your kicking skills?

I think the most helpful things have honestly been my two kicking coaches (NFL vets Mike Hollis and Mike Husted). They are role models, they are mentors. They've taken a chance on me, welcomed me into their homes, even gave me a place to stay while training when financially it was tough. But because of them, I am where I am today. So outside of continuously training (on and off the field), eating right, and staying the course, it would definitely be working with them.

What does your perfect day look like?

My perfect day on the field isn't necessarily a perfect day kicking but having perfect form. When you have a day where it's just effortless. Coming off the foot right, clean rotation, great height. To me, that's a perfect day! Because if you do the form right, chances are the ball is going between the sticks, end zone, or downfield on a punt.

Describe your pre-kick routine and mindset for games . . .

For outdoors it begins once we hit the 50-yard threshold. For arena, I generally will do it the second we get the ball since you're always in range. But I'll generally do three dry runs, smooth steps back and over, and I'll follow my line and envision a smooth ball/operation. When it's time to kick, I run out and take two swings before I line up and go for the actual kick.

What's the one thing you would tell your younger self if you were just getting started?

The one thing I'd tell my younger self is to start training sooner and just stay the course. I battled poor eating and it took me until just about after college to lose the weight I needed to. I wouldn't tell myself 'Well go here' or 'Do this' because that would alter my life drastically and I love the journey I had. So I'd just tell myself to stay the course and be patient.

WHAT'S THE MOST HELPFUL THING YOU DO WHEN YOU FEEL OVERWHELMED OR STRESSED?

This is an important one. Mental health as an athlete is almost taboo to talk about. We're trained and taught to be strong and brush things off. But the most important thing is to acknowledge when you're struggling on or off the field. Kicking wise it's breathing exercises and just focusing on getting through it. Off the field, I talk to my best friend, or I invest in a hobby to keep my mind occupied and at ease! The gym, drawing, playing an instrument, going to the beach, there are so many outlets and we should never be afraid to speak up.

WHO HAS MADE THE BIGGEST IMPACT IN YOUR KICKING CAREER?

There are three people that share this answer. So I'll go in the order I met them. Triple M! Michael Barnard (FDU, Eagles), was my first kicking coach. He was the first person to take a chance on me when I was looking for a coach. He taught me so much on and off the field. We developed an amazing relationship and because of him, I learned the ropes, and it opened doors for the next two people on this list.

Mike Hollis (Jags, Bills, Giants), based out of Jacksonville, Florida, you're guaranteed good times and an experience to learn a challenging and different form. Most kids will come in, be challenged, and walk out, but the form is simple, the form works. Mike and I get to coach camps and travel together as well as work year-round. I've been fortunate to have him in my life as a coach and more of an extended family. Again, I learned so much on and off the field from him, and because of that, it's helped shape me to be who I am today.

Lastly, Michael Husted (Chiefs, Bucs, Raiders). Based in San Diego California, the Husted kicking experience is another amazing opportunity. I've had the opportunity to kick next and alongside Jason Myers and so many others of his caliber. Like Hollis, Husted has kindly welcomed me into his home, and we've shared many meals together as well as just hanging out off the field.

What all three coaches have in common is that they have been more than coaches to me. They've welcomed me into their homes, spent time with me while visiting to train, had meals, shared life experiences, and it's taught me to be who I am, and how to properly carry myself. They have been role models, best friends, family, mentors, and so much more. Because of them, I started coaching and sharing all I've learned with kickers I develop the same relationships with. So to all three Mikes, thank you doesn't cut it but thank you so much.

Favorite breakfast or meal for a game?

Strawberry, banana, peanut butter powder, a scoop of PB protein with a cup of almond milk in a smoothie form! It's light but filling. Prior to a game a small portion of plant-based pasta and a salad will do just the trick!

Favorite workout to develop leg strength and speed for kicking?

Box jumps and resistance band movements! It activates fast-twitch muscles and you use every muscle you would while kicking!

What's your favorite stretch? (It can be static or dynamic.)

This is a rough one! I'm a stretch therapist and have an endless book of stretches. My favorite one involves a wall and a floor. I call it the wall splits. You go in your back, go flush against the wall and move both legs to their most flexible position and I just sit there for about a minute or two. This lets all the blood around me circulate!

Your favorite field goal moment?

I was in Cedar Rapids and it was my second season. It was my first game back towards the end of the season. We went out for a 56-yard kick. Beautiful blocking, beautiful snap and hold. I got all of it but it hit the crossbar. Turns out there was a penalty so we got to rekick from fifty-one. Same thing, BOOM, flew off the foot and right down the middle. That's my career-long. And the fans that caught the ball gave it to me so I have that proudly displayed on my football shelf.

WHO DO YOU LOOK UP TO?

A three-way tie between Mike Hollis, Mike Husted, and Adam Vinatieri. Seeing the snow kick got me interested in kicking, I'd reenact it in the snow and a few years later I began kicking and I had the honor of meeting him. Hollis and Husted because of all they have done for me and the experiences I've had with both of them. I truly don't know what my life would be like without them and without football. But I'm thankful we crossed paths. It's opened many doors, I've learned so many things on and off the field and I truly wouldn't have it any other way.

RAMIZ AHMED

– NFL Free Agent with an interesting story. Walked on to the Nevada football team in 2017 and handled kickoffs. In 2018 he won the field goal duties as well. Was 56% on touchbacks. In 2020 he competed with Pineiro for the starting spot with the Chicago Bears.

INSTAGRAM: @I_M_RAMIZ

TWITTER: @I_M_RAMIZ

WHAT GOT YOU STARTED IN KICKING?

I started kicking because I had some buddies of mine that played football. I had grown up playing soccer but played on a team that was older than I was, so all my soccer friends were in a grade above me. My school friends all played football and nagged me constantly to kick so I eventually gave in around 6th grade and tried it out. The rest was history.

When did you know you had a future in kicking?

I kind of always thought to myself that it was an option, even when I was a kid. I always had a big leg and thought that would translate well to kicking footballs. I have always had kind of just known I could kick successfully at a professional level.

What are the most helpful things you've done to progress your kicking skills?

The most helpful thing I'd say to help my progress in kicking is finding a coach (John Carney) that I jive with and trust. So much of kicking is mental and people move at their own pace (or their environments pace) in terms of maturing. So putting myself in the right environment is what I think has made me progress so much.

What does your perfect day look like?

I love to train so training would be very much involved with having a perfect day, I love kicking and being on the field so that would be as well.

Describe your pre-kick routine and mindset for games.

Pre-kick routine and mindset for games is something that is pretty consistent but has changed as I've matured. I always get a good warm up to make sure I'm feeling nice and loose before kicking and I like to be focused when I kick. My mindset for games is that I know I've done the preparation and that there truly isn't a single kick I can't make or perform. I'm pretty zoned in on game days so there's not a whole lot of thinking going on. Very much a flow state.

What's the one thing you would tell your younger self if you were just getting started?

This is a tough one and is one that I think will be different for everyone but I'd tell my younger self to kick coming out of college, kick in camps in high school, find a coach that I can work with to help me mature. These are all things I didn't do so it's making my route to the NFL much tougher than it otherwise could have been. (And I believe would have been).

What's the most helpful thing you do when you feel overwhelmed or stressed?

The most helpful thing for me when and if I feel overwhelmed or stressed is to meditate or read some books that I know bring me back to the moment. I also listen to people that inspire me (podcasts or interviews) in the moments and it kind of just reminds me that the worst thing is happening in my imagination. It took practice but now it's something that I do by nature.

Who has made the biggest impact on your kicking career?

John Carney has definitely made the biggest impact on my kicking career. He's been around the block and then some and has a great kicking environment and has an unreal amount of knowledge. He's been a great mentor to me and has without a doubt been the largest factor in terms of getting to where I am today.

Favorite breakfast or meal for a game?

For breakfast I like 4 eggs with spinach or some other greens, oat meal, toast, a protein bar and some coffee. If it's pregame meal, I like to keep it light but make sure I have enough in me to keep my energy up during the game. Depends on what is available.

Favorite workout to develop leg strength and speed for kicking?

There are a lot of leg exercises I like to do for leg speed and ball striking. I will say one machine that has helped me a lot throughout my career is the vertimax (can look it up for a detailed explanation).

There's just so much you can do on this machine that translates to healthier, faster, stronger and bigger legs (and core). (Sprints are also very important for leg speed and fitness, arguably the most important)

What's your favorite stretch? (It can be static or dynamic.)

I can't say I have a favorite stretch specifically but I love stretching in general. It's important to keep the body loose and to stretch around 3 times a day. Both static and dynamic are necessary. Very important to stay healthy.

What's your favorite field goal moment?

I don't know if I have a personal favorite field goal moment. I kicked a 30 yard game winner in double overtime in high school against Santa Margarita and that was my first game winning kick so that was a cool and fun moment. Pulling through for your guys is a great feeling and is something I do my best to make happen on every kick. Every made kick or successfully executed kick is a good feeling.

Who do you look up to?

I haven't had many role models in my life and didn't look up to very many people when I was growing up. This has since changed thought and I think it's important to have people you look up to. Roger Federer is someone I idolize, Kobe Bryant was, and Rafa Nadal.

NICK GATTO

— Born with one arm, he has amassed a large track record. All-State kicker in high school, All-American in college, a fourteen-year career in the arena leagues, won All-Rookie team with the Orlando Predators, 1st Team All-Arena two years in a row, and SFC AF2 Kicker of the Year in 2008.

Instagram: @4thand10kickingandpunting

Twitter: @NickGatto

What got you started in kicking?

I started kicking when I was in seventh grade. I would go out to the field at my junior high and I would just start putting my foot to the ball and I was self-taught. I would make a few, I would miss many, but over time I figured out the formula.

When did you know you had a future in kicking?

I realized I had a future during my junior year. I started receiving letters and questionnaires in the mail from colleges and universities and coaches and I realized I possibly had a future. I decided to put the work in and see what my chances were after high school.

What are the most helpful things you've done to progress your kicking skills?

When I was playing the best thing I ever did was finding somebody who could teach me the right way. My coach was a gentleman who was in a wheelchair; he had worked with many prominent specialists and I knew if I wanted to do better, and be better, I had to learn to do it the right way. Learning the proper technique, learning the proper form, learning distance, learning leg swing, learning all the little fine details would help progress my kicking skills.

What does your perfect day look like?

My perfect day when I was playing was when my day was not interrupted by unexpected distractions. Those are things you can't control such as traffic on the way to the facility, another player acting unlike his usual self as a distraction to the rest of the team, a team meeting doesn't go the right way. There really is no perfect day but in a game itself it's when you're able to hit a good clean quality ball: the rotation is perfect, the trajectory, the feeling, the excitement, etc., are all things that would be considered a perfect day.

Describe your pre-kick routine and mindset for games . . .

My mindset would start the night before the game. Everything I did from what I had for dinner, what time I went to bed, what I did before bed, were all things factored into game day. My pre-kick routine consisted of facing my body toward the direction of the uprights I would be kicking at. Walking through that perfect kick in my head as I took my steps. Making sure that my steps were comfortable, my steps were on point, my body alignment, my swing, etc. If everything was correct everything was comfortable and the result is what I wanted.

What's the one thing you would tell your younger self if you were just getting started?

I would tell myself to be patient LOL. Too many kids want instant satisfaction or instant gratification (Instagram for example where they post their kicks for likes) but they don't realize how long and how much it takes to learn how to do this thing correctly. When I was younger and getting started I thought I knew it all but I didn't and even as a coach now I'm still learning how to be better for my players.

What's the most helpful thing you do when you feel overwhelmed or stressed?

The biggest thing that helps me is I decompress and I disconnect. The biggest thing a lot of people forget is how to self-care. Sometimes you have to put the phone down, turn off the TV, go for a walk, go for a drive. Unless you take care of yourself you're going to be burning the candle at both ends and you'll feel that overwhelmed or stressed feeling. The biggest thing that helps to do is a deep breath.

Who has made the biggest impact in your kicking career?

The people who make the biggest impact are the ones who believed in me. The ones who pushed me, the ones who encouraged, the ones who got in my rear or my face if I needed it. There really isn't one specific person, it's all the coaches. Who I have much admiration for and respect are the ones who made the biggest impact because they gave me the opportunities to force me to perform at my best.

Favorite breakfast or meal for a game?

My favorite meal before the game has got to be pasta and sauce with a side of fruit.

Favorite workout to develop leg strength and speed for kicking?

My favorite workout has got to be plyometrics. Box jumps, jumping for distance, pushing a sled: all these exercises in culmination together provided explosion speed and power.

What's your favorite stretch? (It can be static or dynamic.)

My favorite stretch of all for years was when you are standing up and you spread your legs apart and you reach down to your left leg and then you reach down to your right leg and then you reach down the middle. At one point I was able to do the splits: they gave me the best stretch in my opinion for my body.

Your favorite field goal moment?

My favorite moment was in 2002 and my very first game in the arena league. It was my very first kick it was a 48-yard field goal. I was very nervous, I was very scared, and to hear the crowd erupt, enjoy and cheering and screaming and myself jumping up and down after I made it was one of the best experiences ever.

Who do you look up to?

Many people will see one specific person but in reality, the people who I look up to or the person I look up to are those that never quit believing in me. In high school and junior college that's a division one level in the arena league during my pro days there was a culmination of coaches, not just one person that I had much respect for, I admired and I held to a very high standard because of one how they treated me, two how they pushed me, and three they knew the potential I had and they made sure they found a way to drag it out of me to be my best.

WIHAN VAN DER RIET AKA "ROCKETFOOT"

— Current NFL Free Agent with a rugby background. His social media is an online journal of the progression of his technique. He often posts 70+ yard field goals, which he makes with ease.

INSTAGRAM: @ROCKETFOOT

TWITTER: @WIHANROCKETFOOT

WHAT GOT YOU STARTED IN KICKING?

As a South African male, my birth was celebrated with a gift: a rugby ball. Instinctively, I kicked it and never stopped.

WHEN DID YOU KNOW YOU HAD A FUTURE IN KICKING?

I started making a living teaching kicking techniques as a means to continue working on my own craft. I never really knew if I would even catch a break until I got signed in 2021. If I wasn't signed this year, it wouldn't have changed my determination to get signed. To an extent you create your own destiny if you believe, keep on believing, and continue to work on the stuff that matters.

WHAT ARE THE MOST HELPFUL THINGS YOU'VE DONE TO PROGRESS YOUR KICKING SKILLS?

Things changed for me when I met Mike Hollis and started learning the ProForm philosophy.

WHAT DOES YOUR PERFECT DAY LOOK LIKE?

Breakfast, weights/boxing with super loud rock music - cardio with the dogs - Field session in the African sun - lunch - power nap - core/flexibility/balance/stretching - dinner - family time.

DESCRIBE YOUR PRE-KICK ROUTINE AND MINDSET FOR GAMES . . .

Couple of kicks before kickoff, light cardio, and a good stretch. Be carelessly confident. You either miss or you don't. Just focus on technique, don't think about the outcome at all.

WHAT'S THE ONE THING YOU WOULD TELL YOUR YOUNGER SELF IF YOU WERE JUST GETTING STARTED?

I would tell my younger self: Don't buy into any hype. People are trying to make money by selling you. Most of them have no idea what they are talking about and would abandon you before you know it. It's going to be a long road to success, invest in the things that matter. Technique, healthy mind, and healthy body.

WHAT'S THE MOST HELPFUL THING YOU DO WHEN YOU FEEL OVERWHELMED OR STRESSED?

To relieve stress I hike and try to get lost in the bush. The more disconnected from the world the better!

WHO HAS MADE THE BIGGEST IMPACT IN YOUR KICKING CAREER?

By far Mike Hollis.

FAVORITE BREAKFAST OR MEAL FOR A GAME?

I would say I prob carb up the night before with homemade pasta. I don't eat a big meal before a game . . . prob because I'm from a rugby background and that hasn't ended well in the past. Lol.

FAVORITE WORKOUT TO DEVELOP LEG STRENGTH AND SPEED FOR KICKING?

Those are my secrets. ;)

WHAT'S YOUR FAVORITE STRETCH? (IT CAN BE STATIC OR DYNAMIC.)

I do a variety of dynamic and static stretching. I can't name a favorite since stretching is my least favorite part of the day.

YOUR FAVORITE FIELD GOAL MOMENT?

At age eighteen, in 2007 I kicked a 70-yard goal kick at the death [end of match] to win the game for my rugby club at the time, the Police Rugby Club. It was our only win of that season.

WHO DO YOU LOOK UP TO?

I look up to and draw inspiration from many people close to me and some I don't know personally. There are so many incredible individuals in this world, doing incredible things. All you have to do is open your eyes. There are also plenty of stories from the history of my people: how they got to Africa, how they ended up here, and the challenges they faced in the process. Incredible stories of perseverance and determination. These pioneers, who against all odds wanted freedom from English rule and settled in Southern Africa against all odds. It's always inspiring to hear their stories, they had balls of steel. Whenever I'm in a tough situation I always think, "Well at least I'm not fighting off lions, trekking barefoot over the Drakensberg mountains with my family in an ox wagon."

ALI MOURTADA

– NFL Free Agent with experience in the IFL and NAL. His Instagram has countless posts of him hitting 80+ yard kickoffs through the uprights, as well as long field goals that he hits with consistency.

INSTAGRAM: @_ALI_MOURTADA

TWITTER: @HAKUNA_MOURTADA

WHAT GOT YOU STARTED IN KICKING?

I had an incredible love for soccer as a kid. In my neighborhood tho, all my friends played football. So after playing backyard football and enjoying it, my parents put me into Pop Warner football, where I brought the soccer background along with me.

WHEN DID YOU KNOW YOU HAD A FUTURE IN KICKING?

Idk if I ever "knew" that I had a future. But from day one I always believed I could. I grew up in Foxborough, MA so the dream of playing professional football was literally in my backyard. I did have some talent but I was not very decorated in accolades as a kicker. Because of this I always made sure to keep working on becoming better every day.

WHAT ARE THE MOST HELPFUL THINGS YOU'VE DONE TO PROGRESS YOUR KICKING SKILLS?

The best thing I ever did was surround myself with some great kickers. In college, I didn't know any kickers looking to go to the next level so all the work was done on my own. I improved the most when I moved to California for six months and trained with guys who were at a high level. Jason Myers, Kenny Spencer, Taylor Russolino. The atmosphere I was around cultivated improvement in the craft.

WHAT DOES YOUR PERFECT DAY LOOK LIKE?

The perfect day for me is my daily routine. Up at 4:30-4:45 a.m. Train in the weight room from 5:20-6:20. Take care of my clients from 6:40-10 or 11. Take some downtime, either read, journal, clean, eat, power nap. Kick on the field from 4-5:30. Wind down at home with some recovery. Either stretch, compression boots, Epsom salt bath.

Spend time with my family before calling it a night around 9 p.m.

Describe your pre-kick routine and mindset for games . . .

My pre-kick routine is very simple. A solid warm-up to get the body firing on all cylinders followed by one-steps with a focus on ball contact before working my way into full-steps. As for kicks in a game, a few strikes into the net and I'm ready to execute.

What's the one thing you would tell your younger self if you were just getting started?

Do the little things and basics with utter obsession.

What's the most helpful thing you do when you feel overwhelmed or stressed?

These are common emotions. I think the best way to handle these emotions is by doing the work prior. Do everything in your power to prepare and you will be better equipped for times like these.

Who has made the biggest impact in your kicking career?

This is a tough question. So many people have played roles in this journey. From coaches to family to friends. There has always been someone there along the way. I wouldn't have started this journey without the blessing and belief of my sister, Natalie. The opportunity to even make that choice couldn't have been made without the sacrifice of my mother, Samira, and my father, Ahmad Mourtada. I wouldn't have the knowledge of the body and training without my friend Nathaniel Zinni. I wouldn't be the man who can overcome adversity and handle success without my soul mate Yeseña Gutierrez. I wouldn't have the technique and form without my coaches Michael Husted, Sam Watts, Nick Novak, Gary Zauner, John Carney, and Nick Lowery. I wouldn't have developed the belief in myself without my kicking brother Sergio Castillo.

Favorite breakfast or meal for a game?

I like to keep it light. Protein shake with a slow-releasing carbohydrate such as UCAN.

Favorite workout to develop leg strength and speed for kicking?

This is so in-depth that I'd be doing it an injustice to pick one thing. Some tools I use with exercises are tempo, isometric, and end ranges of motion. I will say, having a stable core to shoot the leg from is of great importance.

What's your favorite stretch? (It can be static or dynamic.)

Pigeon stretch and couch stretch are a couple of my favorites. As a side note, we must aim to be strong in positions we are flexible.

Your favorite field goal moment?

At this point in my career, it has to be a game-winner in high school against a top-five opponent in the state.

Other kicks have been memorable. In my freshman year of college, I had the fortune of connecting on a record 52-yard FG. My first professional FG was from 51 yards. These are all great memories to carry with me.

Who do you look up to?

My father. He passed away three years ago. But he left behind wisdom and lessons in my heart that continue to unfold and reveal themselves as I grow. He was a man who overcame and always put his family first. If I can create a family as my father did, that is the greatest achievement. Loving, forgiving, and always there for one another.

JIMMY CAMACHO

— Fresno State alumni, converted twenty-five field goal attempts his senior year to set a single-season school record. Played in the IFL for the Arizona Rattlers in 2019 and is currently playing for the CFL BC Lions.

INSTAGRAM: @MYNAMEJAMESBRUH

TWITTER: @MYNAMEJAMESBRUH

WHAT GOT YOU STARTED IN KICKING?

My friend in middle school was trying out for the high school team and encouraged me to try out. I dragged my feet and didn't really want to at first. I knew nothing about football. I started kicking with the kicking coach and had some natural ability with kickoffs so they convinced me to stay for the rest of the summer.

WHEN DID YOU KNOW YOU HAD A FUTURE IN KICKING?

My senior year in high school I hit a kickoff through the uprights and I had only ever seen NFL kickers do that at the time. Looking back now I realize how rare that is for a seventeen-year-old.

WHAT ARE THE MOST HELPFUL THINGS YOU'VE DONE TO PROGRESS YOUR KICKING SKILLS?

No-step field goals and punt darts.

WHAT DOES YOUR PERFECT DAY LOOK LIKE?

Perfect day is hitting three or more field goals in a game, 100% touchback. Or going 100% in a chart for a combine. That's always hard to do.

Describe your pre kick routine and mindset for games . . .

I just have a generic warm-up. I'll do a lot of no-steps and darts before I start, but that's common. I never do one-step stuff. No-step or full-step for me usually.

My mindset for the game varies. One kick at a time. I tell myself things to boost my confidence mostly.

What's the one thing you would tell your younger self if you were just getting started?

Get good rotation! Hitting ten in a row from thirty-three is more important than hitting five in a row from sixty.

What's the most helpful thing you do when you feel overwhelmed or stressed?

SHEESH! The bad times are terrible in this business. I like to golf and play basketball. Helps me decompress.

Who has made the biggest impact in your kicking career?

My college coaching staff in 2017. They gave me all the confidence in the world to just go out there and cut it loose.

Favorite breakfast or meal for a game?

Cinnamon Toast Crunch is the pregame ritual.

Favorite workout to develop leg strength and speed for kicking?

Front squat or barbell lunges.

WHAT'S YOUR FAVORITE STRETCH? (IT CAN BE STATIC OR DYNAMIC.)

Stretching and warming up is my least favorite thing in the world. I do it out of necessity not pleasure.

YOUR FAVORITE FIELD GOAL MOMENT?

It was a very special moment for me to break my college single-season FG record. I only started one year, so you can imagine what that meant to me.

WHO DO YOU LOOK UP TO?

John Carney and Nick Novak. Both have mentored me in my post-college journey.

MIKE HOLLIS

– Nine-year NFL All-Pro veteran. Was a member of the 1997 Pro Bowl. Holds records for total points, field goals, and field goal attempts with the Jacksonville Jaguars.

INSTAGRAM: @PROFORMKICKING

TWITTER: @PROFORMKICKING

WHAT GOT YOU STARTED IN KICKING?

I played soccer for many years as a kid and always enjoyed kicking the ball. I also played pick-up football a lot with neighborhood friends and decided to play for my eighth-grade "lightweight" team where I was a receiver, defensive back, and the kicker and punter. Kicking was my favorite position and I quickly found a passion for being the best that I personally could be.

WHEN DID YOU KNOW YOU HAD A FUTURE IN KICKING?

I knew that I had a future in kicking the same day I realized my passion for the skill . . . in the eighth grade. However, my definition of "future" at that time was nothing more than knowing I loved the skill and had developed an inner challenge to myself to be as good as I could be, personally. Wherever that took me, I'd be happy and satisfied with.

What are the most helpful things you've done to progress your kicking skills?

As a kid kicking in high school, I was mostly relying on my somewhat athletic abilities to get me by. I was very intrigued with the art of kicking but didn't really know if I was doing the fundamentals correctly. Until I met my longtime kicking coach, Jim Gaetano, I never realized how detailed kicking could be. The most helpful thing I had done was simply to listen to my kicking coach and focus on everything he was teaching me, regardless of what the kicks looked like. This trusting mentality led me to the second-most helpful thing . . . realizing that kicking form and technique was everything, and predominantly responsible for successful field goals and kickoffs.

What does your perfect day look like?

Smooth, fluid, flexible, calm, effortless kicks. I took a lot of pride in doing the same things every day, regardless of how I was feeling physically and mentally. Some days I was missing some of the things I mentioned, but I didn't want the lack of those things to make me change what I was doing while kicking.

Describe your pre kick routine and mindset for games . . .

My pre-kick and mindset routines were pretty simple . . . trust my form. Many times kickers get caught up in trying harder and subconsciously second-guessing themselves in games, which is where you see the great practice kickers who don't perform well in games. My specific pre-kick routine consisted of warming up into the kicking net after my offense crossed midfield. I'd focus on the "feel" of the kick, making sure every practice kick felt solid and my follow-through was natural and forward. This "feel" concept in games, practice, or anytime I'm kicking, is mostly like a "summary" of all the technical aspects of the kick, without actually thinking about all those technical aspects. In other words, if I think about the "feel" of good kicks, my brain will coordinate my body and muscles to repeat that good "feeling" of the kick, without much thought.

What's the one thing you would tell your younger self if you were just getting started?

I'd tell myself "Don't care where the ball goes." Believe it or not, the result of the kicks were not my priority! The proper form and technique are way more responsible for making successful kicks, and if you are too concerned about the result of the kick then you will always revert back to natural athletic abilities and ultimately end up trying to steer the ball through the uprights rather than trusting your form to do it for you. That's where kickers get caught up in second-guessing themselves . . . when they put way too much priority in making the kick. Young kids getting started would never think this way . . . and quite honestly, many experienced kickers won't either.

What's the most helpful thing you do when you feel overwhelmed or stressed?

All aspects of life can get overwhelming and stressful at times. The thing that has helped me the most is to simply get back to basics. Focusing on the problem with issues at hand, and simplifying the situation(s) so that it's easier to control. In kicking, the basic foundations are things that you know and trust and are easy to repeat . . . then move forward from that.

Who has made the biggest impact in your kicking career?My kicking coach Jim Gaetano has had the biggest impact in my kicking career. He is the single-most reason for my nine-year NFL career, as he was not only my kicking coach since high school, he was also like an active agent when it came time for recruiting to the next levels. Jim has taught me everything I know about kicking and he still coaches to this day . . . with me at ProForm Kicking, Jim is the head "Kicking Guru".

Favorite breakfast or meal for a game?

Lots of heavy pancakes and eggs, with a boatload of syrup.

Favorite workout to develop leg strength and speed for kicking?

I have a very different approach to the concept of "leg strength" and speed for kicking. I am a firm believer in high-intensity anaerobic and plyometric types of training to develop great speed and coordination with kicking. For me, kicking is a very quick and explosive motion that requires coordination and flexibility in order to get the best out of me. I'm not opposed to weightlifting but prefer using lighter weights if so because I feel that lifting heavy sets the mind to think kicking is a "power" skill, rather than a speed and coordination skill. One great area of focus in the weight room is the core and hip areas of the body, which assists in achieving the proper technique (firm body position at the plant). The combination of coordination, speed, and proper technique will get athletes the "leg strength" they are looking for.

What's your favorite stretch? (It can be static or dynamic.)

Athletes that are able to do full splits in all three directions will have the right amount of flexibility for the majority of what's needed in proper technique. In addition to the splits, quad stretching and lower back stretching are just as important.

Your favorite field goal moment?

My most memorable and favorite field goal moment was when I hit a 59-yard field goal against the St. Louis Rams in the 1996 preseason. I was only in my second year of my career and had missed a few field goals prior to that attempt and this was a "make or break" moment for me. Making that kick gave me incredible confidence and solidified my position as the Jaguars kicker for the next five seasons. I made thirty of thirty-six field goal attempts that season and was eight of nine in the playoffs in which we made it to the AFC Championship game in only our second year of existence. That 59-yarder in St. Louis was the most important kick of my life!

WHO DO YOU LOOK UP TO?

I look up to a lot of guys . . . guys who have played before, during, and after my NFL playing days. I have a lot of respect for the guys who've kicked and punted for many years in the NFL because I know exactly how difficult it is to play in the NFL. Guys like Morten Andersen, Gary Anderson, John Carney, Adam Vinatieri, Jeff Feagles, Brian Moorman, Darren Bennett, and Bryan Barker to name a few of many.

DARREN BENNETT

– Played in the West Australian Football League (WAFL) and the Australian Football League for five years collectively. Was placed in the 1990s All-Decade Team as a punter. In his rookie season in the NFL, he was second in punting average, and made the AFC Pro Bowl Team.

INSTAGRAM: @NFLAUSSIE

TWITTER: @NFLAUSSIE

WHAT GOT YOU STARTED IN PUNTING?

I had an uncle who was a good Aussie Rules player and he taught me how to kick a ball a long way.

WHEN DID YOU KNOW YOU HAD A FUTURE FOR PUNTING?

I had a lot of knee injuries in Aussie Rules and my strength coaches worked a lot of technique and flexibility, which gave me a good understanding of how to kick. As my legs fell apart for running I strengthened them for punting and then turned my head to trying to make the transition. I won a few long-kicking contests in Australia and it seemed like something I could try.

What are the most helpful things you've done to progress your punting skills?

I had a Chinese tai chi master help me with flexibility and stability that really turned my kick into a punt.

What does your perfect day look like?

Fishing or punting with my son.

Describe your pre-punt routine and mindset for games . . .

I had a great technical coach when I first started in San Diego, Chuck Priefer, who really broke the punt down to the basics, which helped me so much. I would do line and drop drills in pregame, which most NFL punters wouldn't have worked on since high school when they first learned to punt. They would laugh when they saw me doing the basic drills but I knew that, combined with my leg swing and strength, gave me an advantage.

What's the one thing you would tell your younger self if you were just getting started?

It will be frustrating and a struggle at first. Find a coach who can teach you a system of technique and use it every day to create the muscle memory. One day you will grow the body that will take advantage of the good technique you have been taught. Life doesn't always go as you think or plan in your mind. But it will be worth it in the end and you will never be perfect but you will have days where it's awesome and fun.

What's the most helpful thing you do when you feel overwhelmed or stressed?

If you've practiced hard and done the work, trust the work . . . And take deep breaths.

WHO HAS MADE THE BIGGEST IMPACT IN YOUR PUNTING CAREER?

I have had a lot of people help me over my time. My long snapper Dave Binn and my personal protector Terrell Fletcher . . . we were a team . . . we felt like if the three of us did our jobs then we would be OK. John Carney, our kicker, taught me how to be a professional. Chuck Priefer, my first special teams coach. My strength and conditioning professors. Tom Odgers, Chris Jones, Mother Dunn, and Dave Redding.

FAVORITE BREAKFAST OR MEAL FOR A GAME?

Pasta, bananas.

FAVORITE WORKOUT TO DEVELOP LEG STRENGTH AND SPEED FOR PUNTING?

I did a lot of cycling because of my injuries . . . helped strengthen my legs and keep them fast.

WHAT'S YOUR FAVORITE STRETCH? (IT CAN BE STATIC OR DYNAMIC.)

I use a static stretch strap to help me stretch, taught to me by Hall of Famer Morten Andersen. Seated splits. Dynamic-wise I use a bungee system to keep me stable and make sure my leg swing is straight. If I rotate I fall over so it gives me good feedback in my warm-up phase.

YOUR FAVORITE PUNTING MOMENT?

Anytime I messed someone up or made a real football play, like a tackle . . . I broke a guys nose once, Knocked a D lineman on his butt and stripped the ball and caused a fumble. It makes guys realize that you want to do everything you can to help them win.

Who do you look up to?

This will sound cliched but I look up to my son Will who has muscular dystrophy and is my hero in his constant struggle, and my wife Rosemary who looks after him every day.

MATT AMMENDOLA

– Was on the Carolina Panthers' practice squad earlier this year. Led the Big-12 in field goals and points scored in his senior year at Oklahoma State University, making twenty field goals.

Instagram: @mattammendola

What got you started in kicking?

I started playing football when I was eight, along with soccer, and the coach heard I could kick a soccer ball pretty far so he threw me in there in practice and from then on it kind of stuck! I honestly didn't think I was going to pursue football in high school, though, as I was looking to play D1 soccer. Yet, after having a solid background growing up with kicking till I was about fourteen, I tried out my junior year and won the job.

When did you know you had a future in kicking?

When I attempted and made a 56-yard field goal in a game against our rival school during my junior season. From then on, my coaches and teammates told me I could do something with kicking in my future and I decided to run with it and see where it would take me.

What are the most helpful things you've done to progress your kicking skills?

Being disciplined, having a positive mindset, and staying focused every day you walk on that field. When you go out and warm up, be confident in who you are as a kicker/punter. How you approach practice is how you will approach a game. Being tough and having the mentality that you are the best kicker in the country can go a long way. With that, mediating and visualizing are key things I have taken over towards the end of my college career as well.

WHAT DOES YOUR PERFECT DAY LOOK LIKE?

A perfect day doesn't exist. As a kicker, you always have to adapt to new settings and environments and stay ready for anything.

Every place you kick will be different in some way, but it's how you work in those conditions and find your niche on taking any situation you may come across in account.

DESCRIBE YOUR PRE-KICK ROUTINE AND MINDSET FOR GAMES . . .

Staying focused for starters . . . Visualizing the day of and listening to music before the game. When I get out on the field, I like to walk/jog around and get a feel for the stadium. I am locked in and ready to put every ball through the uprights! I continue to build my confidence in pregame and take a few dry swings before I start my dynamic warm-up and then do some static stretching before I start to kick.

WHAT'S THE ONE THING YOU WOULD TELL YOUR YOUNGER SELF IF YOU WERE JUST GETTING STARTED?

Don't give up! As a kicker, you will have ups and you will have downs. I hate to say it but it is true. Some of the best kickers in the NFL have off games and sometimes off seasons, but it is how you bounce back and push through and show not just others, but prove to yourself that you have what it takes to be great and make it. Be patient and stay positive.

WHAT'S THE MOST HELPFUL THING YOU DO WHEN YOU FEEL OVERWHELMED OR STRESSED?

Take a deep breath and focus on yourself. Block out anything around you, regardless if it is in a game or practice, the only thing that you can control is you. Find calmness in your body and realize if you're going through it, stressed, or whatever the case may be, it will get better.

WHO HAS MADE THE BIGGEST IMPACT IN YOUR KICKING CAREER?

I would say my family. The people who will always have my back and support me till the end. They continued to give me hope and confidence that got me to where I am at today to be the kicker and individual I am.

FAVORITE BREAKFAST OR MEAL FOR A GAME?

Eggs, sausage/bacon, toast, banana, coffee, water.

FAVORITE WORKOUT TO DEVELOP LEG STRENGTH AND SPEED FOR KICKING?

Activation and plyometric exercises in the hip flexor and adductors. Rotational movements with bands or light weights. Slow negative and resistance training, mixing in explosive components within the lower half of the body to fire more fast-twitch muscle fibers.

WHAT'S YOUR FAVORITE STRETCH? (IT CAN BE STATIC OR DYNAMIC.)

Dynamic stretch: Frankenstein kicks. Firing the hamstrings and quads, getting the blood flowing.

YOUR FAVORITE FIELD GOAL MOMENT?

My first college field goal attempt, making a 53-yard field goal at home when no one knew who I was yet. I was just in awe being on the field and playing in an atmosphere of over 50,000 people, cheering and screaming your name.

WHO DO YOU LOOK UP TO?

I look up to GOD first and foremost and my parents. GOD has a plan for everyone and for me, looking up to him is an everyday thing as he continues to guide me in the right direction to be the best person and individual I can be. I look up to my parents as well! They have done so much for me from the time I was a kid to now and I wouldn't be anywhere close to where I am today if it wasn't for their help and their support! I love them so much and look to them for everything. GOD and my parents have helped forge me to be the man I am today.

IAN BERRYMAN

– Has played preseason games with the Steelers. Three-time All-Southern All-Conference punter, and best punter in the nation his sophomore year of college.

INSTAGRAM: @IANCBERRYMAN

TWITTER: @IANCBERRYMAN

WHAT GOT YOU STARTED IN PUNTING?

I started playing soccer when I was three years old. I was a goalkeeper growing up and could always punt the ball farther than all the other kids we played against. From there, my dad and I would go out to the field and punt the football casually. Found out I was pretty good at it and the rest is history.

WHEN DID YOU KNOW YOU HAD A FUTURE IN PUNTING?

My second year of starting at Western Carolina, I had an NFL scout tell me, "Keep on track with your progression as a punter and with some luck you'll be extremely successful at the next level." Ever since then, I've been working to perfect my craft and make it my future.

What are the most helpful things you've done to progress your punting skills?

Working with my punting coach, Dan Orner, on body position while I punt and working with my sports performance coach, Chip Smith, who has helped me work on my explosiveness.

What does your perfect day look like?

Punting and working out in the morning, eighteen holes on the golf course in the afternoon.

Describe your pre-punt routine and mindset for games . . .

I've always tried to not overcomplicate things. I try to find my swing line somewhere in the stadium then I tell myself to "Swing easy and let the ball do the work." Saying that has always kept me grounded and allowed me to not overthink things.

What's the one thing you would tell your younger self if you were just getting started?

Work on your flexibility and be more compact with your steps.

What's the most helpful thing you do when you feel overwhelmed or stressed?

Meditation or golf!

Who has made the biggest impact in your punting career?

Dan Orner and Dawson Zimmerman. They have molded me into the punter I am today.

FAVORITE BREAKFAST OR MEAL FOR A GAME?

For me, my favorite pregame meal is a loaded baked potato and fruit.

FAVORITE WORKOUT TO DEVELOP LEG STRENGTH AND SPEED FOR PUNTING?

Band-resisted swings, band-resisted jumps, and high pulls.

WHAT'S YOUR FAVORITE STRETCH? (IT CAN BE STATIC OR DYNAMIC.)

Literally called the "World's Greatest Stretch".

YOUR FAVORITE PUNTING MOMENT?

My first punt in the preseason with the Steelers in 2019 against the Bucs. 66- yard (officially) 5.3+ hang punt.

WHO DO YOU LOOK UP TO?

My dad, 100%!

BRYAN BARKER

– Pro Bowl punter in 1997, and 1st Team All-Pro in 1997. Punted an 83-yard ball against the Jets in week five of the NFL season.

INSTAGRAM: @QUIKKIX

WHAT GOT YOU STARTED IN PUNTING?

I played all sports growing up. It's what we did without the internet, smartphones, etc. Whatever season it was, I played one of the sports . . . football, baseball, cross country, track, golf . . . I think it helped with hand–eye coordination for sure. In high school during football I was a backup QB and starting DB. Our punter wasn't great so I did that too. We won the Northern California 2A Championship but none of us got college scholarships. I walked on at Santa Clara University, as just a punter, and beat out three others to start as true freshman. It was the first time I really trained and practiced as a punter.

When did you know you had a future for punting?

As a senior in college, I could watch the NFL on TV and compare hangtimes/distances to mine . . . I wasn't too far off. I also knew a big stadium, a better field, and a pro long snapper would help! I was determined to give it my all.

What are the most helpful things you've done to progress your punting skills?

Flexibility is key. Most think it is for the motion of kicking, when in fact it is for recovery. Punting is taxing on the body. I was determined to be the ironman of practice punting. I could kick all challengers into the ground with better endurance due to my recovery. I also worked hard to improve all aspects of punting . . . strength, nutrition, psychology, focus, massage, chiro, sleep, etc.

What does your perfect day look like?

Racing a car on the track followed by a sunset dinner cruise on the boat :) In terms of punting, a perfect game is one where my punts were as good as they could be for each game situation: going in . . . coming out . . . directionally away from the returner . . . and always avoiding a blocked punt.

Describe your pre-punt routine and mindset for games . . .

I always went out without pads, before pregame with the specialists, and kicked in both directions from midfield going in, as well as from each end zone coming out. It gave me a feel for the field/footing, and the wind. (I played in some crappy stadiums back then!) I would return to the locker room and dress for team warm-ups. I would also watch the opposing punter and returners to see how they were doing. I punted a lot in pregame . . . which gave me a great place mentally during the game. I felt like I had kicked all over the field already, rather than "Here comes my first punt from this spot."

What's the one thing you would tell your younger self if you were just getting started?

Don't specialize in one sport. Play as many as you can!

What's the most helpful thing you do when you feel overwhelmed or stressed?

In terms of punting, I would always try to avoid thinking too much. I worked hard and kicked a lot all week and my favorite saying when the cameras were rolling was, "Just kick the ball."

Who has made the biggest impact in your punting career?

I grew up over the hill from Oakland, watching Ray Guy. He was known to be an all-around great athlete. Upon making it in the NFL after four years of trying, I was lucky to have Nick Lowery show me what it was to be a professional.

Favorite breakfast or meal for a game?

Usually eggs, potatoes, pancakes, and sausage for early games. Chicken and pasta for late or night games.

Favorite workout to develop leg strength and speed for punting?

Day after Sunday game: 10 x 100 sprints plus weight room (no punting). I always worked out on Tuesdays, even though it was a day off: 10 x hills or stadium stairs plus weights (no punting). Wednesdays: heavy punting day followed by 8 x half-gassers . . . no weight work.

Thursdays: solid punting day followed by 10 x 100 striders plus box jumps and weight room. Friday: light punting and weight room. Saturday: walk-through. Sunday: game day.

I liked the combination of strength and quickness. I came in the league running five miles a day but that did nothing for punting. Half-gassers and hill sprints are awesome.

WHAT'S YOUR FAVORITE STRETCH? (IT CAN BE STATIC OR DYNAMIC.)

Don't have a favorite. I did them all . . . took about twenty-five minutes. It was easy to tell which areas were tired or sore. It was a great time to read something while going through my routine. Don't forget the back muscles!

YOUR FAVORITE PUNTING MOMENT?

So many. Here a few that are different . . . Jaguars: completing a pass in a Monday Night win against Steelers. Jaguars: scooping a ground ball snap at the end of the game and getting the punt off for a fair catch inside the 10, before getting crushed by a Tennessee Oiler (after dislocating my shoulder earlier in the game). Chiefs: two punts inside the 5 in overtime at Arrowhead to help us beat the Chargers and get to the playoffs. Jaguars: 83-yard punt on MNF against the Jets. Packers: 64-yard punt at end of game against Lions to help Packers secure playoffs in 35+ mph winds.

WHO DO YOU LOOK UP TO?

Parents and God. I also respect and appreciate anyone chasing their dreams with confidence and passion . . . always striving to improve while staying positive and grateful.

CRAIG PETERSON

– Has played for multiple AFL teams and was recently signed with the

Albany Empire arena team at the time of this publication.

INSTAGRAM: @CRAIG_PETERSON19

TWITTER: @CRAIGTHELEG19

WHAT GOT YOU STARTED IN KICKING?

It was a random night in Albany, NY. I was hanging out with my friends and we were all watching a Jets preseason game. Jay Feely was the kicker at the time and he missed a few field goals that game but after a missed 50-yarder I blurted out, "These guys get paid millions of dollars to make field goals and miss all the time. I can make a 50-yard field goal!" So of course, my friends being who they are challenged me by saying No, you can't. So it was at that point I told them Let's walk over to Albany High right now and I'll prove it. We did just that and, long story short, I ended up hitting a 50-yard field goal on the first try. After that my friends said Craig maybe you should try kicking footballs. That's exactly what I did after that day.

WHEN DID YOU KNOW YOU HAD A FUTURE IN KICKING?

I had met a kicking coach in Buffalo, NY through a friend from college. It was about a year after my stint at Albany High School. I stayed a week out in Buffalo with my friend and met up with Sam Watts three times during that week. After the third kicking session with him he was shocked to see the progress I had made already and he could see how coachable I was along with my work ethic. He told me if it was possible to move out to Buffalo and work with him full-time and get a part-time job so I could support myself while training. He said he could see me being a great kicker if he was able to work with me more and really focus on my form and technique because the power was already there. That was all I needed to hear from him because I knew I was always going to outwork everybody else. In this case I was going to do everything possible to become the kicker that he saw in me. With that, I knew I had a future in kicking.

WHAT ARE THE MOST HELPFUL THINGS YOU'VE DONE TO PROGRESS YOUR KICKING SKILLS?

Watching film daily and breaking it down, writing things down while watching film to develop new muscle memory in order to be consistent with every kick, and constantly going over the proper form and technique with dry runs.

What does your perfect day look like?

A perfect day as a kicker is going to the field prepared and with the mentality that you will get better TODAY. A perfect day isn't just about being consistent and not missing any field goals. It's about getting mentally better as well. Preparing yourself for that opportunity you'll get when the time comes. It's putting yourself in situations during practice that are game-like so you can be ready for anything. So my perfect day is being better than the day before and being perfect on the field.

Describe your pre-kick routine and mindset for games . . .

My mindset is always the same for games. As for my pregame kick routine, that stays the same as well. I go into every game being positive and knowing I'm going to have a great game. There's no reason to put pressure on myself because I just have to let the game come to me. I always make sure I'm prepared for whatever may come during a game. That's why I always practice game-like situations: so when the opportunity comes in a game, I'm ready for it. Before every game I always do my dynamic warm-up and hit some warm-up balls on each end of the field. I hit a few extra points and a few field goals from the hashes on each upright. I then get together with my snapper and holder and go through a few extra points and alternating hashes for field goals on both sides of the field.

What's the one thing you would tell your younger self if you were just getting started?

I would've told my younger self that it's so important to get good grades in high school because playing football in college is a huge advantage to getting to the next level. Not just that but I would've said you can get a scholarship to a college so you won't have to pay student loans haha.

What's the most helpful thing you do when you feel overwhelmed or stressed?

Yoga. You develop breathing techniques and it improves your flexibility as well. Feeling overwhelmed and being stressed happens. Nobody is perfect but breathing is essential to keeping your stress level down. Also being optimistic and thinking positively helps as well.

Who has made the biggest impact in your kicking career?

My kicking coach Sam Watts has by far had the most impact in my career. He took a kid who never kicked anywhere before, with no high school and no college experience, to the highest level there is: with that being a workout with the Atlanta Falcons. I've also been to multiple CFL training camps as well as being one of the best kickers in arena football. That being said I'm still getting better so to me, being in the NFL is inevitable as long as a GM takes a chance on me.

Favorite breakfast or meal for a game?

Favorite breakfast is a 5 egg omelet with spinach leaves, onions, red peppers, and mushrooms. The best meal before a game is grilled chicken and pasta.

Favorite workout to develop leg strength and speed for kicking?

Dynamic lower body workouts, plyometrics, band work, Pilates.

What's your favorite stretch? (It can be static or dynamic.)

Dynamic stretching is always great, especially before kicking. My favorite though is banded leg raises while laying down.

YOUR FAVORITE FIELD GOAL MOMENT?

I have two. In my rookie season, I hit an AFL season-long 45-yard field goal in Jacksonville. My second was a 56-yard franchise-record field goal in Spokane.

WHO DO YOU LOOK UP TO?

I look up to my mother. I wouldn't be where I am in my career today if it wasn't for her and I wouldn't be the man I've become today if it wasn't for her. She means the world to me and I'm so grateful to have had the best mom raise me and teach me everything that she has.

KENNY SPENCER

– Eight years professionally in the AFL. AFL Kicker of the Year and 1st Team All-AFL in 2012 after setting a single-season record with 138 PATs.

INSTAGRAM: @KENSPENNOW
TWITTER: @LETITRIDE19

WHAT GOT YOU STARTED IN KICKING?

I was training on the soccer field my Jr year of high school. A guy pulled up to the field and approached me. It was the head football coach. He asked, "Kenny, have you ever thought about kicking field goals?" I said, "I mean I've done it horsing around." He said, "Will you kick me a couple?" That was that. The rest was history. I kicked a few 50-yarders for him and he gave me the job.

WHEN DID YOU KNOW YOU HAD A FUTURE IN KICKING?

I went to a kicking camp after my Jr season of high school called the Billy Cundiff Kicking camp. It was the first day. Everyone was warming up getting ready for Billy to come out. This is the first time I actually kicked against other kickers. Now, I'm watching guys and think, Man I can do better than that. Before you know it, I'm at 60 yards hitting nukes with another kid there name Alex Henry, think he went to Nebraska. After I was done warming up, My pops said to me, "Shoot son. You weren't lying, you can kick that thing. We may have got something here." That's when I started taking it more serious.

What are the most helpful things you've done to progress your kicking skills?

Training and keeping a journal of my workouts. My journal was Instagram. I posted a video every session so I had a journal of each day to reflect on, watch my swing. I immersed myself with the form to create the best possible swing my body could make.

What's the one thing you would tell your younger self if you were just getting started?

Get my health on track earlier rather than later in my career.

Favorite breakfast or meal for a game?

Chorizo and egg burrito.

Favorite workout to develop leg strength and speed for kicking?

Plyometric movements like hang cleans, power cleans, box jumps—anything that requires an explosive movement.

What's your favorite stretch? (It can be static or dynamic.)

I stretched before every kicking session with a resistance band.

YOUR FAVORITE FIELD GOAL MOMENT?

My first ever game with the LA Kiss. I hit a game-winner against the San Antonio Talons.

LUIS ZENDEJAS

— All-PAC-10 and All-American in college for making twenty-eight field goals at Arizona State University. An AFL All-Star for the Arizona Rattlers. Has played for various AFL teams and NFL teams during his career.

INSTAGRAM: @ZKICK4LIFE

TWITTER: @ZKICK4LIFE

WHAT GOT YOU STARTED IN KICKING?

When I was in high school my science teacher saw me playing soccer and got me into kicking a football.

WHEN DID YOU KNOW YOU HAD A FUTURE IN KICKING?

After a few years of kicking for my high school team, we won the CIS championship game and we won with a 43-yard field goal. To date that's the only championship my high school has.

WHAT ARE THE MOST HELPFUL THINGS YOU'VE DONE TO PROGRESS YOUR KICKING SKILLS?

Practicing building my leg speed by running bleachers and other explosive movements.

WHAT DOES YOUR PERFECT DAY LOOK LIKE?

When I go 10/10 on field goals and my longest kick is fifty-eight yards.

Describe how you prepared for games when kicking

I had a couple practice kicks from the middle, right hash, and left hash. A few longer kicks and then some onside kicks, pooch kicks, then some long kickoffs. That way when it was game-time, I've kicked all over the field to fully prepare myself.

What's the one thing you would tell your younger self if you were just getting started?

Practice more kicking in general and then practice more snap, hold & kicks. It's much easier to make the kick when the ball is standing still, so working that snap, hold & kick often gives you great preparation for game-time. Practice bad hold scenarios and then practice consistency over long kicks.

What's the most helpful thing you do when you feel overwhelmed or stressed?

I don't feel stressed or overwhelmed, it doesn't exist for me because I go out, kick and have fun. Go out and love what you do.

Who has made the biggest impact in your kicking career?

My science teacher in high school. We developed a kicking block for me to use. He gave me a ton of advice especially when I was transferring from being a soccer player into a football kicker. His help was huge because we only get called out onto the field a few times so it was very helpful to have him as a mentor early on in my kicking career.

Favorite breakfast or meal for a game?

Spaghetti and steak.

Favorite workout to develop leg strength and

SPEED FOR KICKING?

Bleachers and running up mountains (or any big incline runs).

WHAT'S YOUR FAVORITE STRETCH? (IT CAN BE STATIC OR DYNAMIC.)

Setting up five hurdles—three low and two high—going over the hurdle then under, over then under (you can put them high, low, high, and facing one direction go over, under; then repeat, going back facing the same direction).

YOUR FAVORITE FIELD GOAL MOMENT?

Kicking the last-second 43-yard field goal in high school.

WHO DO YOU LOOK UP TO?

Adam Vinatieri.

RECAP OF PROFESSIONAL KICKER/PUNTER Q&A

Every kicker/punter has a specific thing that helps them be the best they can be. While a common theme around strength development was either core workouts for balance, or plyometrics, it shows that the best put a priority on explosive movements.

These guys didn't get to the professional level just on luck. Every single one of them had to put an intense amount of effort in to excel at a high level. They didn't let one day dictate their future, they stayed consistent in their effort and didn't let the highs get too high or the lows too low. Small consistent effort beats inconsistent all out every single time.

14
STRETCHING

STRETCHING AND RECOVERY FROM GAMES

After you are done kicking for the day or the game, you take extra good care of your body. Ice baths will be your best friend in order to help you recover efficiently. Ice baths have been shown to help relieve soreness and muscle aches. Make sure to do adequate stretching throughout the rest of the day to get all the soreness out of your body. It's not fun waking up the morning after a game and being extremely sore because you didn't take care of your body. Do the responsible thing, drink plenty of water, and stretch.

As mentioned earlier, Wim Hof has a meditation style. He also has a stretching method, which works wonders for the progression of flexibility.

Basically all you do is: before you go into your stretch as you would normally do, take (five to ten) very deep heavy breaths, hold the last deep breath in, and then go into the stretch. Go until you feel the need to breathe, then let go, and you will find you can stretch much deeper than you could when you first began.

As a result, That would be one round. Repeat this two to three more times per stretch and you will be able to get a much, much deeper stretch than you could without the method.

Type in, "Using Wim Hof Breathing To Effectively Stretch And Relax Your Mind." on Youtube.

Yoga

Yoga is a great way to tap into your mind, body, and spirit connection. It's a mix of both stretches and workouts blended together. Depending on the style of yoga you do, it then depends on the degree of difficulty you face. There are some yoga classes that are strength-based, some that are more stretch-focused, and some that are spiritual-focused. They each serve a different purpose but all greatly help your kicking.

Kicking is much more synchronized when you are balanced. Yoga will help develop that balance and make you into a better kicker/punter. There are so many different ways to learn yoga. The easiest way to learn yoga would be to simply YouTube yoga videos. A great one to watch is the youtube video "miracle morning yoga by Dashama". Typically, yoga is holding specific positions for a long period of time in order to develop both strength and the stretch of that movement.

Pilates

Pilates is a great way to understand your hips much better. Throughout this book we talked about having neutral hips and this form of exercise is the king to understand that feeling. One of the fundamental ways to understand what neutral hips feel like is to lay on a flat surface on your back. Take your hands and put them under the small of your back. Right now, there will most likely be a little space for you to put your hands underneath that arch. From here, pull your belly button in to engage the core. Your hips are now in a neutral position. This is where you want to be in your start position, and at contact, for both punts and field goals.

Neutral hips are the bulk of what you are trying to maintain during a Pilates exercise. Pilates can be very humbling for those who have never done it before. There are hundreds of different Pilates exercises to help you develop your core strength but more importantly your deep core. That is really where true power comes from. Everyone wants to have six-pack abs but sometimes they have extremely weak deep core muscles. To find out how strong your deep core is, start with your hands under the small of your back in a neutral spine position. Currently, your back should be completely flat to the floor. From there, raise your legs completely perpendicular to the floor while still maintaining a neutral spine. At this point, slowly lower your legs together and see how far you can go by keeping your back completely flat on the surface without it bending or bowing. If you can get your legs from the completely perpendicular position all the way down to the floor without your back moving, That's a good sign that your deep core is strong. If your back bends and disengages, we've got some work to do.

A great video channel to watch for Pilates Is "Coreself" on YouTube.

She's got some phenomenal content on there and one video I really like is the basic Pilates mat workout. This covers the essentials of Pilates in a clear and concise manner. Again, if there is one exercise that you should aim to do AT LEAST three times a week, it would be Pilates. Many professionals attribute a lot of their success to Pilates and it's easy to see why after doing just one session.

Stretching has so many benefits: not only for increasing flexibility, but improving strength and power as well. A good stretching routine can be the thing that takes you to the next level of your game. We will go through a whole stretching routine that you can do daily, but just know that proper kicking stretches almost always revolve around the hips. Nonetheless, we will cover a wide variety of stretches you can utilize whether you're at home or on the field. Enjoy!

Stretches to do at home

For all of the stretches we are about to talk through, all you need is a mat and enough space for you to lay down with your arms stretched out. You should aim to stretch out daily: for at least twenty minutes when you wake up and when you go to bed. As always, drink plenty of water, focus on your breathing to get the most out of each stretch, and listen to your body. We don't want to risk injury so just be smart while you stretch.

The hip flexors serve as one of the most important stretches for a kicker/punter, so that's where we'll start.

Your hip flexors serve many purposes, some of which include:

- Stabilizing the spine and back.
- Providing support to your core.
- Involved in every step you take.
- Generating the power necessary for running/kicking.
- Improving power.
- Increasing speed of leg movement.
- Making you more flexible.
- Reducing stress.
- Lowering back pain.

- Strengthening core.
- Improving mood.
- Reducing pain when sitting.

Where is your hip flexor?

It's located at the top of your femur (the largest bone in the body) and it connects the hips, back, and groin together as one big happy family.

While it may be hard to miss, many people neglect it, since stretching may not be a normal routine for many.

We will go over a few hip flexor stretches you can implement into your daily routine to really get the most out of your body. They will range from beginner, intermediate, and advanced (if there is an opportunity for advanced stretches).

For a deeper stretch, completely flex the muscle you are trying to stretch. This is known as PNF stretching.

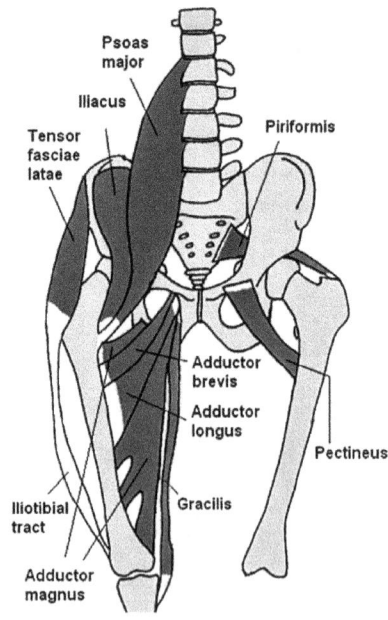

HIP FLEXOR STRETCHES

Lunging stretch
BEGINNER
- Start by simply placing one knee on the ground with the other at a ninety-degree angle in front of you.
- Place your hands on your hips.
- Sink your hips forward towards your front leg.
- Keep a nice tall posture.
- Hold for thirty to sixty seconds as needed.
- Switch sides and repeat.

INTERMEDIATE
- Same steps as above, but raise your hands over your head.
- Reach high and push your hips forward.
- Keep a nice tall posture.
- Hold for thirty to sixty seconds as needed.
- Switch sides and repeat.

ADVANCED

- Knee on ground, front leg at a ninety-degree angle.
- Place your back leg in your hand. (Left leg in left hand; right leg in right hand.)
- Pull the leg up into the glute while keeping a neutral hip position.
- If you want to increase the stretch further, start to move your leg out and away from your body.
- Move the leg into the opposite hand and rotate the other way. (Left leg in right hand; right leg in left hand.)
- Switch sides and repeat.
-

Foam roller/ball hip flexor stretch

BEGINNER

- Lay on the ground with a foam roller.
- Place a foam roller directly on the hip flexor.
- Gently roll three seconds forward, three seconds backward.
- Roll for ten to fifteen reps.
- Switch sides and repeat.

INTERMEDIATE

- Do the same steps as a beginner, only now put little weight on the ground, and put most of the weight on the hip flexor.
- Gently roll three seconds forward, three seconds backward.
- Roll for ten to fifteen reps.
- Switch sides and repeat.

ADVANCED

- Repeat the same setup as the previous two.
- Use a lacrosse ball for a deeper stretch.
- Grab your same leg in your same hand (left to left, right to right), and then move the leg to another hand. (Left to right, right to left.)
- Gently roll three seconds forward, three seconds backward each rep.
- Roll for ten to fifteen reps.
- Switch sides and repeat.

Resistance band hip flexor stretches

For this one, just repeat the "beginner, intermediate, advanced" format, but now it's with a resistance band around our leg.

SETUP

- Wrap/tie the band around a strong structure.
- Put your leg through the loop and place the band under the glute.
- Face the structure and get to a distance where there is resistance but not so much that it slingshots you forward.
- Hold for thirty to sixty seconds as needed.
- Switch sides and repeat.

You can also tie the band around the outside hip, with the resistance going across your body both ways. See the pictures for a reference.

USING YOUR HIPS FOR POWER

Hip flexors are your power center. Learn how to maximize your power from them and they will make you a better athlete, kicker, and a fitter person.

When we stretch our hip flexors, it lowers our pain when sitting, lessens back pain, and loosens us up for peak performance.

Hip-opening stretches are great for increasing your athletic mobility, maintaining power and explosiveness, and improving comfort in day-to-day activities. Proper stretching also helps you sleep better, open the range of motion, and reduce back pain.

For reference, I'm writing this in a hurdler stretch right now. These stretches can be done anywhere that you can get into a deep squat.

Typically, people have weak hips due to negligence. They're one of best muscles to stretch because they do so much for you. After playing collegiate football and asking dozens and dozens of coaches about proper stretching and workout routines, I believe I have found an amazing hip-opening routine.

WHEN TO DO THESE STRETCHES

These hip-opening stretches are best performed first thing in the morning, and thirty minutes before bed.

HOW OFTEN SHOULD YOU DO THESE HIP STRETCHES?

Please do these at least three times per week, but five times or more a week would be the most ideal. That way, you always stay mobile, stretched, and ready to rumble!

It's no surprise that a lot of people have tight hips. We sit for eight hours a day on average and barely get the walking that we need in. Due to excessive sitting, we need to learn how to unlock the power of the hips. We'll quickly highlight the hip-opening stretches routine below, and then get into it:

- Lock and half push.

- Lock and full push.
- Push holds.
- Lock and half-arm reach.
- Lock and full-arm reach.
- Full-arm holds.
- Deep sumo squat presses.
- Deep sumo squat reaches.
- 90/90 get-ups.
- 90/90 walks.

All of these stretches are designed to provide you with the deepest stretch possible for the hips. This is an amazing mobility exercise that within ten minutes will have you well stretched out.

Hip-opening stretches are great to increase your athletic mobility.

The first eight movements will be performed in a deep sumo squat position.

Hip-opening stretches #1 – Lock and half push

- Place one hand on the ground while that elbow locks your knee into place.
- With the other hand, place it on the inside of the knee.
- Press the knee out with the arm halfway extended.
- Repeat this movement ten times.
- Switch to the other side and repeat.

Hip-opening stretches #2 – Lock and full push

This is the same as with half-locks, but fully extends the hand this time.

- Place one hand on the ground while that elbow locks your knee into place.
- With the other hand, place it on the inside of the knee.
- Press the knee out with your arm **fully** extended.
- Repeat this movement ten times.
- Switch to the other side and repeat.

These starter hip-opening stretches get the blood flowing so you can really get the most out of this routine.

Hip-opening stretches #3 – Push holds

These hip-opening stretches are great for stability, and focus on the quality of the movement instead of the quantity.

- Place one hand on the ground while that elbow locks your knee into place.
- With the other hand, place it on the inside of the knee.
- Press the knee out with your arm fully extended.
- Hold this movement for ten seconds.
- Switch to the other side and repeat.

Hip-opening stretches #4 – Lock and half-arm reach

- Place one hand on the ground while that elbow locks your knee into place.
- Take your other hand, rotate, and reach halfway to the sky with your hand.
- Repeat this movement for ten reps.
- Switch to the other side and repeat.

Hip-opening stretches #5 – Lock and full-arm reach

- Same as lock and half-arm reach, only with a full extension to the sky this time.
- Repeat this movement for ten reps.
- Switch to the other side and repeat.

Hip-opening stretches #6 – Full-arm holds

- Place one hand on the ground while that elbow locks your knee into place.
- With the other hand, reach fully to the sky.
- Hold this movement for ten seconds.
- Switch to the other side and repeat.

Hip-opening stretch #7 – Deep sumo squat presses

- Squat down as low as possible.
- Place the elbows on the inside of both knees.
- Put your hands in prayer (beginner) or in a fist (advanced) position.
- Press your elbows out as far as it feels comfortable.
- Repeat for ten repetitions.

Hip-opening stretch #8 – Deep sumo squat reaches

- Get in a deep sumo squat position.
- Place your hands connecting in "hang ten" position (beginner), fists on top of each other (intermediate), or one fist (advanced).
- Try to touch your head to your hand.
- Repeat for ten repetitions.

Hip-opening stretch #9 – 90/90 get-ups

- Place one leg on the ground at a ninety-degree angle.
- Tuck the other leg at a ninety-degree angle behind you.
- In a controlled motion, lift your butt off the ground in a fully upright position.

- Lower yourself back to the ground in a slow and controlled manner.
- Repeat on each side for ten repetitions.

Type in "90-90 Get Down - Hip Mobility Drill" on Youtube for further clarification.

Hip-opening stretch #10 – 90/90 walks
- Do a 90/90.
- While in the upright position, transition the back leg to the front.
- Lower your body down to the ground and repeat.
- Do this for twenty total reps.
-

Again, this can be found on Youtube under, "90/90 walks."

DON'T FORGET TO HYDRATE

After a mobility stretching routine like this, you need to get a lot of water into your system.

These hip-opening stretches are going to really dig deep into the hips and it is important to maintain proper balance in your body.

Aim to drink at least two glasses of water after these hip-opening stretches.

These hip-opening stretches are going to require focus. Due to the power the hips generate, you can see why these stretches are vital to a healthy lifestyle.

When you learn how to relax, you will make your hip flexors more explosive, and your psoas will be happy as well.

Not only using good stretches, but implementing good healthy nutrition, can be a game-changer for your athletic performance. When paired with the proper football-kicker workouts, you will maximize distance.

Workouts for kickers will challenge you to use muscles that are specifically for kickers. Follow these football-kicker stretches to become a better version of yourself and dominate the field!

You can improve these stretches by pushing 1% harder each day. The angles at which you stretch can help as well.

To add to the hip stretches, we will cover some of the other ways you can stretch your entire body out.

One of my favorite stretches to do can be done anywhere where you're able to sit crisscrossed. Simply take one of your legs and prop it up on top of the other leg. You should have one leg on the floor and the other leg supported by the leg beneath it.

This stretch is great because you can get not only your hips but your oblique muscles, which are the side core muscles of your body. The leg that's on top can get really stretched out just by leaning from side to side. After about two minutes, switch legs and repeat the same slow side-to-side rocking motion.

I like this stretch so much because I can do it on the bed, on the couch, watching a movie, playing video games, while meditating, and so much more. The versatility and effectiveness of this stretch make it so beneficial. I'm writing this book in that stretch as we speak.

Another really great stretch is working on your splits. This can be done either with legs apart and reaching down the middle, or with one leg out in front, and the other leg back behind you. Either way, you get an incredible stretch on your legs while you are hanging out around the house.

Just by holding the splits for five minutes a day, by the end of two weeks you will easily be able to see a dramatic improvement in not only your flexibility but in your power during your kicks. If you ever feel like the pain is too much while you're holding the splits, really focus on your breathing—as it will help you maintain and get deeper into the stretch.

For added resistance to the splits, consider holding a lightweight kettlebell in your hands to really upgrade the stretch. But for this, be sure to use a lightweight kettlebell to prevent injury.

Throughout the stretch, the pain might feel pretty intense. But it's good pain, so make sure you focus on taking in ten deep breaths. Eventually, you can aim for twenty to thirty deep breaths.

ADDING WEIGHT TO STRETCHES

There are some instances where you can use weights to increase the stretch you are doing. One great example is practicing the splits both front and sideways by holding a light kettlebell (ten to fifteen pounds) overhead or close to your chest.

While it can take some time to get to a point when you're holding weights while you're stretching, this will definitely simultaneously help both the strength and flexibility of your muscles.

Please consult with a professional before doing these, because we don't need anyone to end up in a hospital because they tried to do the splits with a hundred-pound kettlebell. Start with a light weight that isn't overwhelming, and as you get stronger you can increase the weight in five-pound increments.

My personal favorite method of getting a deeper stretch is through the Wim Hof Method. What you do is take about ten deep breaths, and on the last inhale you hold it and go into your stretch. When you feel like you want to exhale, breathe out, and take a rest. This allows proper blood flow into those muscles that need it the most. If you feel tight in one part of your body while holding your breath, lean into that and hold that stretch.

Another really great way to guarantee deeper splits in ten minutes is to stretch normally for thirty seconds, flex the muscles that are being stretched for ten seconds, then release the stretch for twenty seconds. That will be one round; then repeat that again for nine more sets. By flexing the muscle, you trick your brain into thinking the muscle you're stretching is not the one you're working on. So your brain relieves the pressure and pain in your mind and puts it on other muscle groups. The stretches will move around a lot of lactic acid, so make sure you properly hydrate to keep your body energized. After an effective stretching routine your body might feel tired. Hydration is king!

The other two ways you can get a deeper stretch is by using either resistance bands or weights. (But please consult with a doctor if you have any pre-existing medical conditions or injuries that can limit your range of motion.) These will add additional weight or resistance to stretches, though please only use a weight that is comfortable and won't risk injury for you.

Grabbing a loop resistance band can add resistance to a large variety of leg stretches. Some stretches you can add resistance bands to include:

Put your leg up in the air and wrap a band on the bottom of your foot to pull towards you. These stretches really get a lot of tension out of your legs. As mentioned earlier, they are great when you anchor them into a supporting structure.

Another really good one to do is to anchor a medium-strength band to the top of a pull-up bar, loop it around your outside hip, and lay on the ground on your back. You should be in a butterfly pose, or as close to one as you can, while on your back. The resistance band should now be fully flexed above you.

Then take a light-weighted plate and put it on your inside leg area, pushing the knee down. This will open up both the inside of your leg and the hip, since the weight is pushing your leg open and the resistance band is pulling your hip up. It's almost counterbalancing itself to open up your leg in both places. It's a phenomenal stretch when done properly.

As you progress, you can start upgrading the resistance band weight, as well as the plate itself. Make sure the band is not too heavy, to the extent where you can't lay down on the ground. You also want to make sure the weight is not so heavy that you can't pick it up off the ground. Anywhere from a thirty-five- to a forty-five-pound plate will be more than enough to do this stretch.

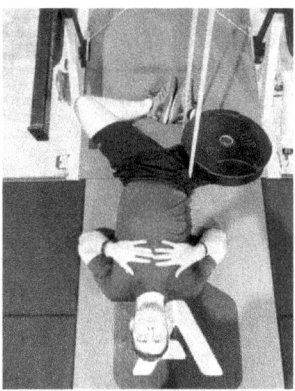

RECAP OF STRETCHING

- No matter what, stretch for at least five minutes a day.
- Stretch on the floor, on your bed, in the bathroom, on the roof. Get. It. Done.
- Splits are a great bang-for-your-buck stretch.
- Use light weights to progress your stretching.

15

WARM-UPS FOR PRACTICE AND GAMES

STRETCHING ROUTINE TO DO FOR EACH PRACTICE AND GAME

Now that we've covered every stretch, it's time to put the pieces together and give you a concrete plan to warm your body up before practice and games.

First things first, we will start with a static stretch. Hold each stretch below for fifteen seconds:

- Feet together, touching toes.
- Right leg over left leg, touch your toes.
- Switch legs.
- Legs apart, touch the ground.
- Legs apart, hold your right ankle.
- Switch legs.
- Right leg forward, left leg back, keep your knee off the ground and get in a deep lunge. Push your hips forward.
- Put the back knee on the ground, sink your hips forward, and put your arms in the air.
- Repeat on the other side.
- With one leg forward and one knee on the ground, put your back leg in your opposite hand and rotate your leg, hitting a stretch on all sides.
- Take that same leg that's back and put it in the opposite hand. Continue rotating and stretching out all sides.
- Repeat that stretch on the other leg.
- Now sitting on your butt, put one leg out in front of you, then

cross your other leg across your body. From there, take your opposite elbow and put it on the outside knee of your crossed-over leg. Turn and twist your body away from your crossed-over leg, stretching out your back.

• Without changing anything else, curl that straight out in front of you and under your butt cheek. Now hug your knee, making sure you stretch out all the parts of your back.

• Repeat this movement on the other side, with the opposite leg stretched out and the non-stretched-out leg curled under your butt cheek.

DYNAMIC STRETCHES FOR PRACTICE AND GAMES

Dynamic movements are simply your adding in motion to get more of an active stretch. These stretches should be done for practice, game-time, or even at home. Typically, dynamic stretches should be done after a static stretch, to get your blood moving and ready for kicking and punting movements.

Some great stretches for the hips are:

High knees

Drive one knee up as high as you can while using your opposite arm to come up to your cheekbones; and, as that knee goes down, the other knee comes up. Make sure your arms are going from cheekbone to pockets in perfect running form. Keep your posture tall; and drive your knees up for speed, not for distance. (You're not trying to cover a lot of ground, you're trying to get as many reps in as you can within ten yards.) When you reach ten yards, jog for another ten yards, and then face the same direction and just do high knees backwards.

Butt-kickers

While keeping a neutral spine and hips, swing your heel up to your butt cheek. Keep your arms pumping as, if you were running. The goal of this drill is not to cover as much ground as possible as fast as you can—the goal of this drill is to get as many reps in the ten yards as possible. After reaching ten yards, jog another ten. Now, facing the same direction, do butt-kickers back.

Leg holds and reach

Hold your left leg in your left hand and reach up with your right arm to the sky, and switch legs. Repeat this for ten yards and jog the remaining ten. It's important not to take steps in between each rep– You're wanting to maximize each individual rep and get the most out of your stretches.

Open the gate

With your feet together, take your right leg and rotate your hip up and out, away from your body. Then skip into your left leg and hip, opening up and away from your body. Repeat this for twenty yards and come back.

Close the gate

Do the opposite motion as you close the gate. Simply rotate your leg and hip up and in towards your body. Make sure you're getting a full range of motion on both movements.

Knee hug and pulls

Take your left knee up into your chest while keeping your other foot flat on the ground. Sink your hips forward, and really get a full range of motion going through the stretch. Go for ten yards and jog for ten. Repeat going back.

Pigeon pulls

Grab your left leg in both hands. Make sure your leg is at a ninety-degree angle, with the foot going across your body. Pull up and towards yourself while maintaining a nice tall posture. Every step is another rep. Go ten yards and jog for ten yards. Repeat going back.

Legs spread, leaning side to side

With your feet together, start the motion by swinging your leg out in front of you downfield, landing facing the sidelines. From there, lean from side to side: putting a stretch on your inside leg and groin. From there, swing your opposite leg out in front of you, facing the opposite direction. Repeat this movement for ten yards and jog for ten yards. Repeat going back.

Backpedal reach-backs

For this drill, face the direction opposite of where you're going, lean your body forward and reach your leg back as far as you can. Drive off of the leg that's in front of you to get a nice pace going backwards. While moving backwards, for each step make sure it is really reaching back and that you're maintaining an athletic position. Go twenty yards downfield and back.

Broad jump

With both feet shoulder-width apart, bring your hips back, get in a loaded squat position, and reach behind you with your arms. Now, all at the same time, drive your hips forward, push off your legs, and pump your arms forward—to jump out in front of you. Land gently on your heels and try not to move after you land. Repeat this for ten yards and back.

Toy soldiers / Frankensteins

Keep your legs straight and your arms straight out in front of you at chest height. Now, each step you take, swing your leg up as high as you can. Just maintain a nice tall posture and don't crunch over in order to give yourself the illusion that you're swinging higher than you actually are. Do ten yards of toy soldiers and then jog for ten yards.

Toy Soldiers / Frankensteins with a bounce

You will still maintain straight legs and straight arms, but the only difference is you are now adding a bounce for each step. You should have a nice rhythm to you, and should smoothly go downfield for twenty yards. Do the same thing coming back for twenty yards.

Alternating lunge holds with a twist

Put one leg out in front of you so it is at a ninety-degree angle. Sink your hips down to the floor, keeping a controlled posture with your body and arms. Then rotate both left and right to stretch out your hip flexors and core. Come back to center balance and take another step out in front of you. Make sure you're not taking small steps in between each stretch. Gather your balance, and go right into the next step without taking mini steps. Go for ten yards and then jog for ten yards.

Spidermans

This one is fun. Put your hands on the ground in front of you in a fully extended position, and bring one of your legs up to your shoulder. (So, for example, I would bring my left leg all the way up to my left shoulder, keeping my other leg all the way back in a stretched-out position.) While staying low to the ground, take your right leg and put it all the way up out in front of you, and move towards that leg. At this point, your left leg should be fully extended back behind you with your right leg up to your right shoulder. Do this for twenty yards and come back.

Bound for height

Using one leg, drive off the ground high and reach with your opposite arm as tall as you can. As you land, repeat the motion with the other leg and arm. The goal is to spend minimal time on the ground after you land. Once you land, quickly explode up and get as high as you can. The higher you go the better. Go twenty yards downfield and back.

Bound for distance

This is essentially an exaggerated running form. Each step you take should be the longest stride you can have. Really reach your leg out in front of you and try to cover as much ground as you can between each step. Go twenty yards downfield and back.

Sprint for ten, jog for ten

Get in a ready stance, load some power in your legs and drive off your front leg, bringing your opposite arm up to your cheekbone. Sprint for ten yards, and jog the remaining ten yards. Do the same thing coming back and you're all done for the dynamic stretches.

Staying warm during games

Football games tend to be longer than your practice sessions. Typically, you might practice for about an hour and a half to two hours and then go home. In football games, it's very common for them to last upwards of three to four hours.

In comparison: when practicing kicking on your own, you might kick maybe forty to sixty times max; while in a football game, you will kick significantly less but you will need to be warm throughout, so that you're ready for anything. A really good rule of thumb is: the second your football team crosses the 50-yard line, start getting ready. Do about two to three kicks into the net to stay fresh. When the time comes that you actually have to attempt a field goal, you're more than ready. Also, if it's been a significant amount of time and nothing has really happened in the game and you're just sitting around, take a few kicks in order to keep your legs loose.

You're teaching yourself bad habits if you sit for a large majority of the game without keeping your legs fresh. By the time your team gets into a position to kick a field goal, if you've done nothing to prepare throughout the game, you're setting yourself up for failure. Stay fresh, and stay ready to get some points on the board.

Likewise, as a punter, when your team gets the ball, practice one or two punts, and do about five drops with good form. When it gets to second down, practice one to three punts and then just start visualizing a perfect punt. At third down, get with your long snapper or someone: to throw you some footballs so you can practice your drops with a snap. Just be smart about it, there's no need to tire your leg out. Being a punter is more predictable than being a field goal kicker. You know that when fourth down shows up your time will be called. As a field goal kicker, the defense can return a fumble for a touchdown and it can really throw some people off. Just make sure you're paying attention to the game and staying ready. You owe it to the team to give it your best. Be enthusiastic, cheer everyone on, and be a valuable part of the team because they need you.

RECAP OF WARM-UPS FOR PRACTICE AND GAMES

- You practice like you play—do everything will full effort.
- How you do one thing is how you do everything.
- Get as much work in with your snapper and holder as you can.
- Stay fresh. You could be called at any moment; be ready.

16
WORKOUTS

The first thing that needs to be said about the workout section is that you have to be using controlled movements in a safe manner to avoid getting injured. It's better to use the perfect form with lighter weight vs using heavy weights and thereby ruining your form, risking injury, and being out for weeks or months at a time because you wanted to impress someone.

For the first portion of the workout session, we will include specific workouts and days of the week to complete them in; and then the second section will be an expansion on most of the exercises and the ideology behind them.

The workouts in this section will be completed during the off-season, and preferably after you kick—since your legs will already be warm from your kicking session.

For all of the weighted workouts, be sure to be explosive on the way up and slow and controlled on the way down. This both works your fast-twitch muscle fibers and maximizes your stabilizer muscles. At the same time, it's important to know that we don't advise lifting weights to a point where it's too heavy to explode up. Every now and then you can challenge yourself with the heavy lifting day, wherein you do your one-rep max for three sets or something of that nature, but it's not as beneficial for kickers to focus on super heavy lifting. Focus more on explosive functional movements at a lighter weight, so you can develop your fast-twitch muscles. Most of the workouts will be more of a functional movement that will be related to your actual kicking motion in some form or fashion. That being said, we have certainly included traditional lifts—as they are great for developing overall strength.

One thing to note is that, when training to get faster and stronger as a kicker, the way to go is to train those movements (and any related ones that replicate those motions) with resistance. So, throughout a workout, have, "Is this going to make me a better stronger, faster, and more explosive kicker/punter?" in the back of your mind. If the answer is no, find an alternative that DOES help you. Granted, anything is better than nothing—but I would be baffled if someone told me wrist curls relate to kicking/punting in any way.

When doing the workouts, it's important to know that you have to want to properly warm up in order to not only reduce injury but increase athletic performance. Oftentimes, people want to go straight into the workout. Please do not do that. It's no different than someone starting a manual stick shift car and, without even changing gears, them flooring it to go the maximum speed.

Warming up and working out is a gradual progression that has some big benefits when they're paired together.

A great warm-up routine for the gym:

- Hang on a pull-up bar or something similar for ten to fifteen seconds.
- Hold a pushup at the top position for ten to fifteen seconds.
- Get on the ground, face down, and stretch your hips, arching your head to the ceiling to stretch your abs for fifteen seconds.
- Raise your hips to the sky and stretch your back (aka the downward dog pose in yoga) for fifteen seconds.
- One slow squat, held at the bottom for ten to fifteen seconds.
- One burpee.
- Five jumping jacks.
- One pull-up.
- One pushup.
- One "dive-bomber pushup" (aka "Chaturanga Dandasana" in yoga).
- One slow squat to the ground and up.
- One burpee.
- End this cycle with five jumping jacks.
- Repeat the cycle.
- Now—doing two repetitions of each exercise, each set followed by ten jumping jacks—repeat the cycle.
- Now, doing three repetitions of each exercise, each set followed

by fifteen jumping jacks.

- Repeat the cycle with this pattern until reaching five repetitions and twenty-five jumping jacks.

After warming up, repeat the movements in the actual workout with extremely lightweight to just get used to the movement as well as work on muscle memory. Do one warm-up set at a lighter weight per exercise to get your muscles ready for the specific movement.

Weight room off-season workouts

These are going to be good just to get a general layout of a weight room session. Later on, we will describe more kicking/punting-specific workouts, but the below gives you a practical workout to do on your own. It follows an upper–lower split for the workouts:

Monday

- Decline crunch (3-4 sets of 12-15 reps).
- Front barbell squat (3-4 sets of 4-6 reps).
- Back squat (3-4 sets of 4-6 reps).
- Box jumps (4 sets of 8-10 reps).
- Deadlift (4 sets of 8-10 reps).
- Dumbbell lunge (3 sets of 10-12 reps).
- Leg press (4 sets of 8-10 reps).
- Leg extension (2 sets of 10 reps).
- Seated leg curls (2 sets of 10 reps).
- Standing raise (3 sets of 12-15 reps).
- One hundred-yard sprint (10 sets).

Tuesday

- Hanging leg raise (3-4 sets of 12-15 reps).
- Incline dumbbell press (3-4 sets of 8-10 reps).
- Dumbbell bench press (3-4 sets of 8-10 reps).

- Dumbbell shoulder press (3 sets of 8-10 reps).
- One arm side lateral raise (3 sets of 8-10 reps).
- Weighted bench dips (3 sets of 10-12 reps).
- Overhead dumbbell triceps extension (3 sets of 8-10 reps).
- Concentration curls (3 sets of 10-12 reps).
- Forty-yard sprints (15 sets).

Wednesday

- Plyometrics on the field
- Squat jumps (3 sets of 25 reps).
- Frog sit-ups (3 sets of 25 reps).
- Standing broad jumps (40 yards, 3 sets).
- Sumo walks, using a small resistance band (30 yards, 3 sets). [Start on the goal line with your right foot forward, keeping tension in the band. Once you get to the 30-yard line, go back with your right foot forward, and repeat this for 2 more sets.]
- Bicycle sit-ups (30 forward, 30 backward).
- One-legged squats (25 each leg, 3 sets).
- Scissor kicks, laying on back feet (6 in off the ground for 60 seconds).
- Sumo squat jumps (25 yards, 3 sets).
- Crunches (3 sets of 25 reps).
- Plyometric jumps (25 yards, 3 sets). [Jump side to side; when you land, pause then jump back: looking for more side distance than forward.]
- Hurdle jumps (30 seconds as fast as you can for 3 sets).
- One hundred yard sprints (10 sets).
- Supermans, lying on stomach (10-second reps, 10 sets). [Lift legs and arm off the ground and flex your back.]

Thursday

- Side bridge (3-4 sets of 12-15 reps each side).
- Front barbell squat (3-4 sets of 4-6 reps).
- Back squat (3-4 sets of 4-6 reps).
- Box jumps (4 sets of 8-10 reps).
- Deadlift (4 sets of 8-10 reps).
- Dumbbell scissor jumps (3 sets of 6-8 reps each side).
- Leg extension (2 sets of 10 reps).
- Seated leg curls (2 sets of 10 reps).
- Standing calf raise (3 sets of 12-15 reps).
- Stadium runs (15 reps). [All the way to the top, and walk down as your rest.]

Friday

- Decline crunch (3 to 4 sets of 12-15 reps).
- Weighted pull-ups 4 sets of 8-12 reps).
- Lat pulldown 3 sets of 8-10 reps).
- Seated cable row (3 sets of 8-10 reps).
- Bicep circuit (6 sets of 8-10 reps).
- Upright barbell row (2 sets of 8-10 reps).
- Barbell shrugs (2 sets of 8-10 reps).
- Single-leg box jump (4 sets of 10 reps each leg).
- Two-mile run. [At an aggressive but not all-out pace.]

Saturday

Pool workouts

Pool workouts are great both to condition you and get a functional movement that relates to kicking/punting. The beauty of pool workouts are that, when you're finished, you can simply dunk your head in the water to cool off. But when it's all said and done, practicing your kicking/punting motion in the pool will increase your range of motion and strength/leg speed.

- Do 3 sets of 25 reps each of:
- Kicking/punt swings.
- Leg raises (outward).
- Leg sweeps (across the body).
- High knees.
- Butt-kickers.
- Knees-to-chest jumps.
- Hip rotations (outward).
- Hip rotations (inward).

Sunday
- Stretch and recovery.
- Walk/run two miles to keep the legs fresh and active.

To pair with the workouts above, it's also important to have a set ab-circuit routine. This is going to be Pilates based, so it will develop your deep muscles that are used the most in kicking; but it will also help the muscles that everyone can see (recti abdominis). So you can get your beach body muscles, as well as your kicking muscles, worked out. It's a win-win!

Pilates circuit

- One-minute plank.
- Plank with leg raise (20 total reps).
- Slow mountain climber (20 total reps).
- Body saw (15 reps). [For added burn, take one leg off the ground.]

- Bear holds (30 seconds)

- Tabletop holds (30 seconds)

- Bicycle Crunches (30 total reps)

- Pilates hundred

- Bird dog (20 reps)

- Pilates scissor kicks (20 reps)
- Double-leg stretch (20 reps)

- Repeat for 2 more sets.

A proper leg workout increases the distance a kicker or punter generates per kick. It can also condition the leg to last longer during practice, games, and the season as a whole. Working out is really just making your muscles uncomfortable—and, through stress, they grow and get stronger.

When a kicker uses momentum to get through a ball, the entire body becomes a useful part of the kick. Eventually, all of the power for the kick gets used with strong legs and an efficient swing.

A good football-kicker workout places a lot of the focus on developing functional strength in the legs.

Developing functional strength in the legs takes time, but it is better to have strength in the legs than only relying on ball contact and everything to be perfect in order to make the kick. When strength is paired with a great foot-to-ball contact, and excellent kicking form, great things happen.

STAYING MENTALLY TOUGH FOR THE LEG WORKOUTS

Far too often, people think they can get through something by "sort of" doing the activity. When doing a challenging activity, do it with the full intent of accomplishing it in its entirety.

Do not tell yourself, "Okay, since I got to the gym late, I can skip the last exercise." You better superset and work out with a sense of urgency. However, the best way to get your leg workouts in, or any workouts for kickers in for that matter, is by being disciplined.

If that means going to the gym earlier to account for the rush at the end, then so be it. Likewise, we make excuses all the time as to why we do not accomplish our goals. We make excuses in our minds about why it does not work out. Prepare for the workout so that you're ready when the time comes. Failing to prepare is preparing to fail.

Box jumps

Stand in an athletic position, with your feet shoulder-width apart, at a comfortable distance from the box.

When you are ready to jump, drop quickly into a quarter squat, then extend your hips, swing your arms, and push your feet through the floor to propel yourself onto the box.

Don't "stick" your landing. Instead, envision the way cats land when they jump from something—you, too, should try to land this quietly.

The beauty of box jumps is that they are so amazing for creating an explosive baseline for the legs and their power. Through box jumps alone, a kicker develops the fast-twitch muscles necessary for hitting farther field goals.

Again, kicker exercises place high importance on functional, explosive strength.

While they work on power, control becomes just as important. The box jumps have many variations as well. A kicker can do one-leg box jumps, sprinting form, high knees touching the box, or even weights with a box jump.

As time progresses, the legs naturally get stronger. Adding weight progressively needs to happen as it improves leg strength exponentially. Once you can do box jumps at or above hip height pretty regularly, consider introducing ten-pound dumbbells in each hand to add resistance. Through progressive overload, the legs properly get challenged—which then allows our body to flourish and grow!

Jumping lunges

The weight for this exercise needs to be one that both challenges you and allows you to get fully off the ground for the target reps.

For example, if you decide to do three sets of sixteen (one rep would be each jump), then, by the third set, there should be no problem getting off the ground by rep ten.

Football-kicker workouts need to challenge your explosive endurance more than raw strength. Since our motions are so explosive, a kicker workout program needs to be done the right way. Train explosive, fast, and smart!

Tire flips

Tire flips are amazing for developing hip strength and explosive speed. It is a very functional movement for kickers and I would highly recommend it! You can get a great workout in by going one hundred yards down the field and back. Or, if you want to break it up, do fifty yards for four sets. Music or podcasts will be your best friend during this because they get you in the zone. Equally, if you like to go deep in your own head, don't play anything and rely on yourself for motivation. There are some very simple steps involved in making sure you have a successful tire flip:

- Keep a tall posture.
- Grab the tire firmly, with both hands under the tire.
- Drive from your legs.
- Explode with your hips, to get an extra push.
- Finish the flip at the top with your arms.
- Repeat.

Squats

Oh yes, enjoy these—squats are among the best and least most fun to do in the gym. When doing a squat, some basic tips must be brought up in order to maximize growth. The closer the legs are together, the more the quads get worked. Likewise, the farther away they are, the more the hamstrings get worked. By all means, if you can do the splits while holding weights on your back, do it, and film it. Jujimufu became famous for this, but we highly recommend against trying anything like that. When performing a squat, engage your core, keep your back straight, go all the way down, drive from your heels, and lock out at the top. You want to make sure you're going all the way down in your squats. A deep squat has been shown to increase knee stability, so it might actually help you to go deeper. Also, you can work on technique more since it'll be harder to do a deep squat as opposed to a parallel-to-floor squat. Drive from your heels, since that's where the power comes from. You risk injury trying to push off your toes. You might consider wearing flat shoes, like Chuck Taylors, or going barefoot for some of these more demanding push exercises that need a flat surface to push off from. You get a more stable connection between the foot and floor when using flat shoes or going barefoot. The squat does many things for your legs; one result being that it creates a strong foundation for your body to perform at its highest level. So stay strong and squat on!

Goblet squats

The granddaddy of mobility exercises, the goblet squat provides so many benefits.

You might be asking, What is a goblet squat?

Well, friend, the workout digest boils the goblet squat into three main benefits:

It's the best squat variation for beginners.

It improves posture by strengthening your core.

It's one of the best mobility and activation tools for the lower body.

When doing a goblet squat, the load becomes much lighter: placing an emphasis on form and technique. This needs to be a focal point for every kicker everywhere—form and technique have become widely overlooked!

Goblet squats, when done correctly, create incredible growth. They are great for the core, hips, legs, lats, and—of course—glutes.

Jump squats

Oh gee . . . this has to be one of the most rewarding and challenging exercises available. When done right, the quads, hamstrings, hips, and core get torched in this exercise.

A great trick is to keep it simple. Just try to explode off the ground. If doing a barbell squat jump, put the bar on the back, put the thumb on the side where all the other fingers rest. That way, the shoulders do not get hinged or hurt.

The proper form allows the body to fully utilize the muscles necessary for the maximum workload. Do the movement carefully but with intensity, so you can maximize distance on your field goals. Make sure to use a weight that allows you to explode off the ground, and gives you enough range of motion to go all the way down in the squat.

Stadium runs

Stadium runs are a fantastic way to build explosive leg strength. It builds the quads, hamstrings, hips flexors, core and calves. All of these muscles are used in kicking and punting so it is a great exercise to incorporate into your workouts. They are a lower impact exercise than jumping or running so your joints will thank you in the long term. Since they are so simple, you can get a great workout in just thirty minutes. Run all the way up, walk down as your rest, and repeat. When doing stadium runs, aim to skip every other step so you're having to explode up and out each time to get to the next step. Stadium runs alone are such a great exercise that you could do them exclusively and see an increase in height and distance on your kicks within a month. Once you can do them with relative ease and want to up the challenge, throw on some leg weights to add more resistance. Make sure the weights don't weigh too much that you are compromising form in your running. One to three pound leg weights are plenty as they will add a noticeable amount of resistance to your workout. Towards the end of your weighted stadium runs, you will definitely notice the difference they make. Try it for yourself and be careful not to fall because falling on stadium runs doesn't exactly scream "i'm an athlete"

Broad jumps

The beautiful thing about the broad jump is that you can motivate yourself to push a little harder each rep. In essence, it is simple: stand in one spot, then jump as far forward as you can. When you land you have a clear vision as to how far you went. On the next jump, you can try to outdo the jump prior. The broad jump, if done properly, improves explosiveness, acceleration, power, and control.

Since it creates so much power in such a short time then sees you having to stop immediately after jumping, it works on your stabilizer muscles and fast-twitch fibers.

Much like kicking, broad jumps take place within a few seconds. Doing them before, during, or after kicking can help fire up the muscles needed for kicking.

Just be careful jumping with running shoes on, as they may not grab the turf as much as football kicking cleats might.

If you are short on time and need some effective leg workouts, doing some jump squats with or without the bar, broad jumps, and goblet squat jumps will get your body moving in the right direction.

Leg-weight swings

The leg-weight swing needs to be utilized more. Many kickers do not understand the importance of functional strength.

According to Antoni Luke-Akagi: "Functional strength training is the practice of motion against resistance, with an objective of improving a participant's ability to perform a specific athletic activity."

The functional strength of leg-weight kicking swings will undoubtedly improve range of motion, strength, and fast-twitch fibers. By using the exact movement kicking is, then adding weights, the body has no choice but to get stronger.

Personally, I use the Wizard leg speed weights. (formerly known as EMVP Leg Speed Weights.) They are incredible and definitely help me in terms of increasing my explosiveness when I kick. The leg weights come with half-pound weights so you can either have little resistance (allowing for a slight resistance kick) or, for the wild people, five pounds of weight per leg. This may not seem like a lot, but five extra pounds definitely add significant resistance to each and every movement you do. (Just note: using all five pounds for each leg makes it hard to mimic the kicking motion with a ball. It would be best to do five-pound swings without a ball; but two-and-a-half pounds and under should allow for an adequate range of motion with a ball.)

These are great for warming up, kicking/punting, working out, stretches, and even daily activities. Every now and then, if I feel guilty for overeating on the weekends, I will strap these bad boys on and walk around the neighborhood.

Another side note is that the interior grips the leg pretty good, so either wear pretty high socks or get a little sweat going on the legs BEFORE you put them on. They might pull a few leg hairs, definitely not fun. But at the same time, no pain no gain, so you decide.

The Wizard leg speed weights in action

Front squat leg workouts

This exercise, when done properly, creates a lot of core, quad, and overall flexibility. Since the bar goes in the front, the body goes deeper into the squat position.

WARNING: the front squat is made for those tough enough to withstand the challenges of having the weight in front. This exercise hits the quads almost twice as hard as the back squat.

Do this exercise with complete knowledge of how to do it. The bar can either rest on the clavicle bone with your elbows pointing away from you, or with your arms crossed. When the arms cross, the weight stays on the shoulders. If you put the weight on your deltoid muscles, raise your elbows as high as you can go in order to relieve pressure from your wrists. You are also able to balance the weight easier from the elbows being up. Whichever weight hold position feels more comfortable, do that.

Develop your own leg workouts

When doing leg workouts, make sure the exercise focuses on different parts of the leg. Doing too much of anything can lead to bad things happening: so make sure the focus remains on progress, not overdoing one thing.

Keep the workouts in balance—your body will thank you.

Hip workouts

While there are endless workouts designed to strengthen the hips, there are only a few that are known to fully benefit a kicking motion.

The hips are one of a kicker's highest priorities. By utilizing the hips, a kicker engages the elastic power when the leg kicks a ball. When the leg makes contact with the ball, a lot of power must be generated in order to make the ball travel a great distance. Therefore, by strengthening the hips, consistency goes up, and so does power.

Deadlifts

The deadlift is often referred to as the king of exercises. Deadlifts utilize almost every main muscle in the body: your hips, hamstrings, quadriceps, upper back, traps, forearms, and core. Therefore, the proper technique needs to be in order for there to be no injuries.

Start with the legs slightly wider than shoulder-width apart. Then, bending from the legs—NOT the back—grab the bar. While keeping the back straight, lift from the LEGS, and push your hips through as you finish the rep.

An upright position maintains power. (Injuries typically happen when the back begins to crunch, bend, and become parallel with the ground.) As time goes on, weight should be increased. If a kicker keeps the legs closer, the quads become more challenged. As a result, the wider the legs go the more the hamstrings are developed. This wide stance is also known as a sumo deadlift.

Rep range for maximum growth

There should be a weight-to-rep range ratio relative to the goal you are trying to achieve.

Low weight, high reps: the more you condition your muscles. While, with the higher weight, lower rep range, the stronger your muscles become. With kicking, try to strike the balance between lightweight and heavy, especially for deadlifts. It should be challenging to you, but light enough so that you can explode up. It should be light enough for you to be able to slowly lower the weight on the way down. Six to eight reps per set is ideal for deadlifts. Since we can lower more than we lift, put extra emphasis on the eccentric (lowering phase) of the exercise. It should be a one-second explosive movement up, a one-second pause, and a slow-but-controlled movement down for three seconds (simply because it becomes enough time under tension for the muscles to get endurance in while still working on the fast-twitch muscle fibers).

Another way to target these muscles is by exploding through the motion. The stronger you become, the easier it gets to perform a movement that was once much more difficult for you. Therefore, you are able to incrementally increase your strength by progressively improving the weight you're lifting. I would recommend staying on a weight until you can complete that exercise without going down in the amount you are lifting. For example, if you are deadlifting 225 pounds, and you can do four sets of ten fairly easily, the next time you do deadlifts, start with 235 pounds for four sets of ten. Keep lifting that weight until you can go at least two gym sessions in a row on that weight, then increase the amount again to 245 or even 255. The point is to slowly work up the weight while still maintaining great form and explosiveness.

Walking lunges

These are great for when you want to build endurance and functional strength. That is the importance of being an athlete: functional and practical strength takes priority over physical strength.

However, the upward movement is different with this form of lunge. All the focus is on the forward leg, with all the muscles of the forward leg contracting maximally in the attempt to stand straight again. One needs stability while performing this exercise.

Power cleans / Hang cleans / Clean & press

The power clean is a technical but extremely beneficial workout. Much like a deadlift, start with the bar on the ground, back straight. Firmly grasp the bar with the hands; then, using the legs, lift the bar off the ground, and thrust the hips forward. Using that momentum, keep the bar going straight up, towards the clavicle bone. Start with a lighter weight, as this will allow you to work the form correctly.

When the bar is chest height, drop down, and aggressively shoot your elbows under and around the bar. This lets your palms go from facing down to facing towards the sky. A proper power clean works the quads, hamstrings, hips, core, arms, and some chest. By starting the bar resting at hip height, this is now a hang clean.

The purpose of the hang clean, like the power clean, is to target almost the entire body. Now, since you are starting from hip height, the deadlift portion does not take place. Therefore, the main focus of this lift is the hips. The hips are the power source for making the bar explode up into the chest area. Having explosive hips will only improve the experience of this workout.

Also, if you (like most people) want to take this exercise a step further, follow along! When the bar gets to the resting position on the clavicle bone, use your arms and legs in unison, and press the bar up over the head. The bar then goes back down: either to the floor if you like to throw weights around (I do); or to the clavicle, hips, then the floor.

This workout targets most if not all of the fundamental muscles, making it a great go-to for kickers. Due to the fact that kickers use their whole body to kick, using workouts that do the same is in their best interest.

Sprinting workouts

Sprinting never gets old. It will always remain an incredible way to get more explosive hips while lowering your body fat as a result. Sprints have many alternatives: shuttles, circuits, suicides, kneeling get-ups, head start sprints, and the most simple, distance sprints.

As most of these may be a new term for many people, we will quickly address each one so you can better understand them.

Shuttle sprints

Shuttle sprints involve from a target distance of, let's say, a cone ten yards away, then back to the start. This way, the main objective becomes quick turns while maintaining control.

Circuit sprints

Sprint circuits are simple in theory but far harder when you begin. A circuit starts with the kicker running either an obstacle or a distance the first time, and then using that time as their base. For example, time yourself running fifty yards. Give yourself a forty-five-second break, then go back the other way, trying to beat your previous time. During your rest after the sprint, do five pushups to up the challenge.

Another way to do a circuit sprint is to give yourself fifteen minutes to do as many sprinting rounds or obstacle rounds as possible. While they will obviously work the body, sprints work the mind too—in pushing your body to keep going when there is little left in the tank.

Suicide sprints

Suicide sprints are a staple in almost every category in sports. They clearly separate the conditioned from the out-of-shape players. This exercise begins with the kicker placing target areas at increasing distances away from them.

For example, the first cone is five yards away, then ten, then fifteen, then twenty . . . all the way up to forty. Run to the five-yard cone and back, then ten and back, all the way up to forty and back.

Or, if you wanted to work the sprints more, lessen the cones between: making it less cardio-intensive, and more high-intensity. (For example, placing the cones at ten-, twenty-, thirty-, and forty-yard lines.) However you want to do it is fine: just make it challenging.

Kneeling get-ups

Kneeling get-ups begin with you on your knees; then, in an explosive motion, drive your legs from under the knees, land on both feet, and sprint. You should aim to sprint for at least twenty yards, to get a lot of reps in without completely tiring yourself out fast. This isn't a conditioning drill as much as it is an explosion and quick acceleration drill.

Head start sprints

Head starts simply work on using momentum to go from an already-moving position to a full-sprinting one. This is mainly for when you want to work on the sprinting portion itself, not the start from zero. These are also great for a time when you simply want to work out your explosive movements while in motion.

Distance sprints

Longer-distance sprints are beneficial in their simplicity. Typically one hundred yards is a perfect distance to cover. Likewise, the break can be a walk twenty yards downfield and back. When you get back to the starting position, restart immediately. On that same note, adding in a timed run can be a great way to track your progression.

Use a stopwatch to see how fast you are sprinting. This way, you are challenging yourself to beat your previous time. Not only have you run that fast before, but you know you are capable of doing even better since you have already done it previously.

Keep your body tall, make your leg strides long, try to have all your energy go forward in front of you, and try not to sway your arms to the side.

When the body works efficiently to get you to the destination, injuries are avoided, and progress becomes exponential. Likewise, when kicking, using your body on the kick makes your job easier, since it gets to work more for the essentials like ball contact, power, and swing path. Your body when kicking can be your biggest obstacle or your best friend. These sprinting workouts focus on delivering maximum results through maximum effort. If you are going at 80% you should expect 80% results.

Resistance-band workouts

Resistance bands are a great workout for the kicker who wants to develop the fast-twitch muscle fibers in their legs. Through consistent work, those muscles become stronger, faster, and more explosive in the kick. Therefore, even if the kicker does not hit a great kick, the strength they have developed will help them have a better chance of making it.

Developing the fast-twitch fibers takes time; but, with consistent work, it can be done. There are hundreds of resistance-band workouts to choose from. The main purpose is to work on the muscles that are weak, making the whole leg balanced and strong.

Fifty resistance band field goal swings, punting swings, and sprint motions are a great place to start. The ankle strap resistance bands are best here. Simply anchor these to a door and do your swings that way.

What is the core?

The core of your body consists of many muscles that, when working together, make the body more efficient, in control, and stronger overall.

There are the muscles everyone sees: the recti abdominis. Then there are the muscles under those, which make your stomach "pop" more: the transverse abdominis. On the sides, the obliques make your balance better when in kicking position. When a kicker leans, they need to balance out far enough away from the ball as to generate any sort of power.

Through proper body positioning and balance, the sweet spot gets hit consistently. Having both great ball contact and consistency will result in more made field goals.

This graph below shows all the muscles I would not be able to pronounce, so please enjoy it.

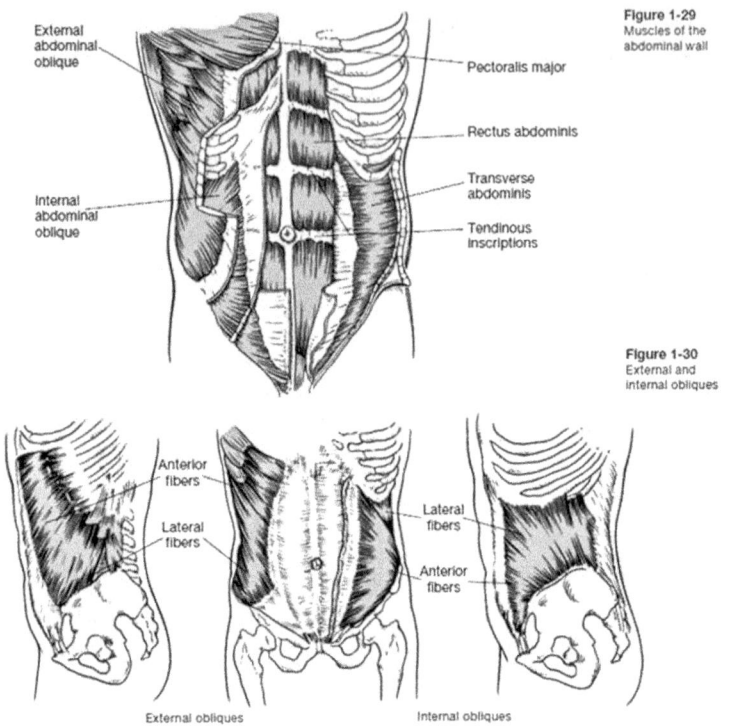

Figure 1-29 Muscles of the abdominal wall

Figure 1-30 External and internal obliques

Gym lovers

"Workouts" simply mean dedicating time out of the day to getting better at something by exerting physical effort. The people who have the greatest on-the-field kicking performances have these as a result of two things: either they are genetically gifted (3.1% of the NFL kickers, or simply one-in-thirty-two) or they just work extremely hard at their craft.

If anyone does a quick Google search on the undrafted kickers, they will see that they put in an absurd amount of time in the weight room. One such example of an undrafted kicker/punter who put in his due diligence in the weight room is Steve Weatherford. He basically lives there.

His leg workouts alone are longer and more intense in one day than some players' are in a whole week. He needs to be a character everyone follows on social media.

In terms of core workouts, Pilates has been proven to give kickers and punters the most bang for their buck.

In his book, Return to Life Through Contrology, Joseph Pilates (the founder of Pilates) presents his method as "the art of controlled movements, which should look and feel like a workout (not a therapy) when properly manifested. If practiced with consistency, Pilates improves flexibility, builds strength, and develops control and endurance in the entire body." Through controlling the movements through various core workouts, a kicker and punter become strong and flexible, and have control of their body.

"Control equals power", as most kicking mentors will mention. The benefits of Pilates are incredible. From betterhealth.com, below are some of the benefits of Pilates (a number of which we have already gone over—yet we simply want to hammer the point home):

Improved flexibility and stretching.

- Increased muscle strength and tone, particularly of your abdominal muscles, lower back, hips, and buttocks (the "core muscles" of your body).
- Balanced muscular strength on both sides of your body.
- Enhanced muscular control of your back and limbs.
- Improved stabilization of your spine.
- Improved posture.
- Rehabilitation or prevention of injuries related to muscle imbalances.
- Improved physical coordination and balance.
- Relaxation of your shoulders, neck, and upper back.
- Safe rehabilitation of joint and spinal injuries.
- Prevention of muscular injuries.
- Increased lung capacity and circulation through deep breathing.
- Improved concentration.

- Increased body awareness.
- Stress management and relaxation.

Core workouts with a pull-up bar

The pull-up bar remains a great way to develop real core strength, since there are no supportive elements to help out.

A great core workout for kickers is the hanging leg raise. Go to the nearest pull-up bar, or anything to hang on that is sturdy. Now, with the feet together and straight, raise them all the way to the bar. This would be the advanced version. The intermediate is to raise the legs to hip height. The beginner version is to keeping the feet together still, and simply raise the knees to hip height (or chest height if you want to get wild and crazy).

The pull-up bar challenges the body to use the whole core and all of its strength. So making the core as strong as possible becomes an important matter for getting better at any other lift. When the core gets stronger, other workouts get easier as well.

Another pull-up bar workout starts by holding the legs at hip height. With a strong core, keep the legs straight out in front. Also, when the legs are straight out, move the legs like a scissor, either vertically or horizontally. This way, the muscle groups get hit intensely. Consistently hitting the muscles in variations is how growth happens.

Core workouts with a yoga ball

The next fun core workout or exercise starts with your finding a yoga ball. Get in a pushup position, point the toes, and place them on the top of the ball. Now, the simple way to do this exercise is to start with the legs together and then raise the knees to the chest, before going back to the starting position. This exercise targets the stabilizer muscles, so that when the kicker gets into the ready position for kickoffs or field goals, the muscles are prepared for the movement.

The variation to the yoga-ball exercise above is to only bring one leg to the chest while the other hovers over the ball. Then, after both sides have been hit, bring both legs to the chest. Again, by adding variation to the exercise, the body does not have adequate time to adapt to the movements. As a result, the body becomes stronger as it adapts to the harder and harder exercises.

As pictured above, another exercise to challenge the core using a yoga ball starts by laying on the back. Holding the ball in the arms raised above the head, move the legs towards the ball. Grab the ball with the legs, and, with the ball now in the legs, lower it to six inches above the ground and repeat. This becomes a yoga ball V-up. Keep the hips in and the core tight and make sure the form stays good. It is better to do the exercise perfectly ten times than it is to do it one hundred times the wrong way.

Using the core for a kick

I hope it is understood that the core is a vital part of any kick. Having a grasp of how to use the core to work for you will become an incredible tool. There have been professional kickers who use their core so well that it gets to be obvious that they do lots of core workouts.

But what do we mean by this?

When kickers have a low backswing it means their hips are in the right spot. This allows for maximum power and accuracy as they hit the ball.

The important part of kicking comes down to the little things. Body positioning is an integral part of making kicks at an 80% rate. When the nerves are so high that a kicker cannot think, they have to rely on their fundamentals.

That means their training on how their body is at contact, and keeping it simple, become fundamental things for a lot of kickers to know in order to make their kick almost automatically.

When simplicity meets power, that becomes a conversation of professional status.

How to use the core during the kick

Exercise helps the body understand how to work in stressful environments. The harder you push yourself in the weight room, the tougher the body gets.

- Engage the core pre-kick.
- Use the core to feel your weaknesses.
- The core should be acting like a whip as the kicker plants their

foot. The core should be tight and stable.

Some of these are hard to grasp in a single bullet point, so we will definitely cover them in more detail.

First, the weight room builds the body. Then, the field uses that growth to utilize it and prove that the hard work is paying off. By engaging the core at contact, the kicker activates the muscles needed for kicking. This pulls the hips in to engage them on the kick as well.

Using the core during a kick can have an immediate impact on your power. Imagine the body works as a series of levers and pulleys. The core is the central piece of the whole mechanism: if one thing isn't working optimally, the whole system breaks down. The core keeps everything together, so that the body can work for you and not against you. So imagine, when we kick a ball: our butt sticks out; our core becomes disengaged; and the ball loses five to ten yards, since our body is not using our glutes or hamstrings as much as it would if the hips are pulled in. If the core is not activated during the kick, it can actually hurt more than it can help, since we are losing a lot of power in the lower body with disengaged hips and core.

How do we solve this problem of utilizing the core during the kick?

When the kicker gets in the ready stance, get the core to engage. As you approach the ball, make sure it remains tight; and afterward it can become loose. This way the hips activate, allowing for maximal whip action. Again, the best kickers make their body work for them and not against them. The core has always been such a crucial part of kicking, and only now are people starting to uncover its potential.

Final tips for the core workouts

- Keep stretching the core.
- Use it to have good posture.
- Strengthen it, and it should reduce injury.
- Find ways to continue to challenge it as time progresses.

As you can see, there are a hundred ways to put the work in to benefit yourself, but none of this advice works unless you do. You've got to be willing to put in the work necessary to come out the other side a champion.

Oftentimes it can be hard just getting out of bed in the morning. Those who rise to the occasion and put themselves out there are the ones who find more success in the long run. It's not about doing good two days in a row. It's about consistently showing up and giving it all you have, so that, come the end of the day, you can lay your head down and know you put in the work necessary to get better. I'll take a consistent effort in showing up over someone who goes all-out for three days and then stops.

RECAP OF WORKOUTS

- Functional and plyometric workouts should be your staples.

- For each movement you do, make your goal to be explosive but controlled.

- Add resistance to your kicking motions (leg weights, pool exercises, cables, resistance bands) for an effective strength-builder.

17
TOOLS TO HELP KICKERS AND PUNTERS OUT

TOOLS TO IMPROVE YOUR KICKING

Throughout this book, we've talked about all the tools to help you on your kicking/punting journey. In this section, we will cover some of the most beneficial tools you can utilize to help you kick anywhere where that you have three yards of space. Some of the best items you can use to improve your kicking will be broken down into three sections:

- Technique.
- Mindset.
- Workouts.

If you are wanting to view the links in this section, they can be found at kickersofearth.com/resources

1. TECHNIQUE
Kicking nets

Kicking nets are going to help you when you want to get that extra work in at home. Oftentimes there will be something you will want to work on, and having a kicking net will give you the ability to solidify some adjustment you're going through. Depending on the weather, you can either set it up on a patch of grass in the yard or on a field. This way, you get a realistic feel of the grass as you kick with your cleats on. At the same time, you are able to kick into the net and not know where the ball goes: which is actually a really good thing, since we're really only working on form and technique here.

On the other hand, if the weather is bad or it's getting dark out, you can always set the net up in the house or garage, on a surface that will allow you to land on your plant leg safely. (We don't need anyone slipping on their butt as they attempt the kick—be careful and safe.) Also, when kicking inside, be smart and don't go 100%. Your tempo and speed should be 50%: simply make sure you hit a clean ball with a swing straight through the target zone.

When kicking into a net, this is a great chance to practice the rope drill, as mentioned on p78.

2. MENTAL

Bullet Journals

Bullet journals are perfect for a lot of different situations: the first simply being because you want to get your thoughts down on paper. These can be either good thoughts or bad thoughts; the point is you are able to effectively express your emotions, their coming straight out from within your thoughts. This is an amazing way to calm yourself down or make yourself extremely excited—it really just comes down to the type of message you're going for. Another huge plus is how, since the pocketbook is so small, you can take it anywhere you feel.

A really good way to use this is before, during, and after your kicking sessions. This way you can look back on it in a few months and see what you were doing when you were at your best, or at your worst. Recording as much as you can gives you a history of how you were thinking during specific days and how that related to your kicking. The more detailed you can be the better, so you can get into the deeper parts of your brain—the true authentic self.

Kicking apps

Kicking apps are a great way to record your kicking sessions. Essentially, after each kick, you go into the app and record the result, and therefore, after about ten sessions, you will have a really good idea of where your weaknesses lie. As such, you are now aware and can now fine-tune your weaknesses to make yourself a more confident, well-rounded kicker. Two of the most helpful kicking apps out there are Kick Tracker and Simple Kicking.

The Kick Tracker app is going to chart each of your kicks across your session. You simply enter the distance of your field goal; whether you made the kick, or whether you missed it (wide left, wide right, short, blocked); and then repeat for the next kick. It also has a section for kickoffs and punts.

Simple Kicking is a much more detailed app: factoring in the wind, the types of field goal posts you're kicking on, which side of the field you're kicking from, the trajectory, and a whole lot more. It's a very detailed app, which even gets down to how you feel after your kicking session. As for when we were talking about journaling your kicking sessions, this would be an amazing app for that. I highly recommended Simple Kicking to all kickers who want to see a statistical breakdown of their kicking session so that they can improve on their results.

Meditation apps

Personally, I recommend Headspace, Insight Timer, Ten Percent Happier, and the Wim Hof Method app. They all have their own benefits.

HEADSPACE

This is the best app for beginners. It has really easy-to-understand animations and a very simple interface. For anyone who is just starting out on their meditation journey, Headspace should be your go-to.

INSIGHT TIMER

Insight Timer has the most amount of meditations on the platform. It's more of a community, where hundreds of different instructors can submit their methods. There are over 70,000 meditations on the app and it shows no sign of slowing down anytime soon.

TEN PERCENT HAPPIER

Ten Percent Happier is an amazing app for those who have experience with meditation and want to go a little bit deeper into that space. They cover some more advanced topics and it's more of an educational experience as it goes through thoughts in the mind and what triggers certain responses to make you act that way. There is also a wide variety of lessons and courses to choose from.

WIM HOF METHOD

Personally, this is my favorite as it's just so much different than traditional meditation. There are significantly fewer lessons, but why need 10,000 different meditations when two or three will get the job done in a more effective way?

His app is simple: there is a section on meditation, cold therapy, and breathing. I had been meditating for over two years when I came across Wim Hof and his methods, and since then I have yet to find any meditation that gets anywhere close to the experience you have after only three rounds of breathing.

He also utilizes cold showers, which are a huge benefit to the human body – but he teaches you all of that in his app. He's a little off-the-wall, but he holds over two dozen records for things like the world's longest time in an ice bath, running a marathon in a desert without water, and climbing Mount Everest in nothing but just shorts and shoes.

(DISCLAIMER: Please do not try any of these at home. These are just to solidify the point that he has tapped into the brain in a way that not many people can do. And he's teaching it to everyone who wants to listen.)

Acupressure mat

Lastly, the mental portion of kicker tools will be the acupressure mat. This is simply a soft mat with thousands of little plastic spikes—aimed at reducing inflammation and lower back pain, and aiding in extensive relaxation. It's great to just lay down on it for about twenty minutes and recharge your batteries.

For the first few minutes, it can be a little uncomfortable. But, as you stay on it longer, you start to sink into the pieces, and before you know it you don't even feel them and you can simply focus on your breathing. The breath is such an important tool for meditation, especially when you're going through a slightly uncomfortable moment. Take a second or two and just pay attention to your belly expanding and falling during each in- and out-breath.

3. PHYSICAL

Fitness apps

I bet you're a bit like me . . . going to the gym and having an already-set routine makes your life so much easier—yet, oftentimes, you lose that little extra push because you feel like you're doing the same thing over and over again. And so it's important to do workouts that you enjoy, but which also make you feel like you're making progress.

JEFIT will be extremely helpful for you to track and journal your workouts. If you have just had a breakthrough lifting day, at the end of the workout there is a note section: so that you can write that down and describe how you feel. It also tracks how much total weight you've lifted. So, if you did eight sets of eight reps of one-hundred-pound explosive squat jumps, your total weight lifted for that workout would be 6,400 pounds. It provides you with a visual at the end of the workout to show exactly how much weight you just lifted. It's actually really cool to know that you beat your previous lift by a whole five hundred pounds, or lifted over 30,000 pounds for the workout. It then makes you want to do even more than that next time. And that's the beauty of these workout apps—they help you push yourself to the limits you are capable of hitting.

Kettlebells

According to Livestrong.com, "Kettlebell swings are initiated with a powerful hip thrust using your glutes and hamstring muscles. In weightlifting, these muscles are, in conjunction with your lower back, referred to as your "power zone" as they are strongly involved in virtually all lifting, running, and jumping movements. Using a heavy kettlebell for low-rep sets will improve your muscular power."

Since the kettlebell is more of an endurance movement than a strength-building one, it acts as a great ten-minute workout when you are short on time.

Be sure to maintain good posture, as that remains the focus of the swing. Good form results in great power and mobility. Keep your back straight, and hinge at the hips. This is not a squat; the hips come back and explode through. The kettlebell will come between the legs and, after exploding the hips, the weight should naturally come up to your chest. The important thing is not to use your arms on the swing if you simply want to work on the hips.

If you want a full-body workout, drive the hips and bring the weight up over the head. The appropriate weight should be light enough as to where the natural momentum should bring the kettlebell up over your head.

Kettlebells are an amazing way to improve your hip mobility, strength, and explosiveness. Every single kicker in the world should be using kettlebells to increase their strength. Doing so develops the entire posterior chain: almost all of the muscles used for a field goal or punt. The important thing is to make sure the form and technique are spot-on, as to maximize its benefits.

It's important not to drop your legs down into a squat as you lower the kettlebell in between your legs. All the power should be coming from your hips, not your legs. To drive the point home—it's a hinge movement, not a squat movement.

Go to YouTube and type in "Kettlebell swings . . . You're doing it WRONG". To see a full detailed explanation of the proper kettlebell swing form.

[NB: This is the Russian version; the American-style swing sees you extend your arms up parallel to your head in a full-range-of-motion swing. (Those are also great for working on your arms and shoulders.) But, just for the purpose of getting the fundamentals down, swinging the kettlebell up to hip or chest height is more than enough.]

Massage/Lacrosse balls

Using a massage or lacrosse ball is a great way to pinpoint a muscle that needs to be worked on. If you want a softer way to massage your muscles, start out with some tennis balls. And if you want to pinpoint a muscle further, use some golf balls. When you use these to stretch out your muscles, it will get pretty intense at times, so make sure to breathe accordingly. But this entire time, while stretching your body out, just remind yourself that this is making you better and this is improving you as a kicker and punter. For the muscles in the upper body, utilize a wall to stand up and roll against it. If you want extra force, you can simply just lay on the floor to roll out the muscles.

Foam rollers

For a larger muscle group, consider using a foam roller. Those foam rollers with the bumps in them apply a little bit more pressure to the muscles being rolled out. If you're going to focus on developing your body, you might as well get a higher-quality tool for it. They're all relatively inexpensive, and will end up helping you in the long run since you won't be nearly as sore having used one.

Massage sticks

These used to be a big favorite of mine since I could do a majority of my stretching while on the couch or sitting in bed watching a movie. Massage sticks are fairly simple: you just hold both sides of the stick and roll on the portion of the muscle that needs attention. In order to work your upper body, it's best you get a partner to roll it out for you. Nonetheless, it's another great tool to help you stay ready to go.

Massage guns

A massage gun is hands-down the most effective tool you can get from the money that you spend. Not only will it stretch out any muscle that you need on your body in an extremely convenient way, but it's also the most portable (alongside a massage ball). Depending on the model you buy, massage guns have varying levels of speed that you can apply to the muscles. The slower speeds tend to be best when working on extremely sore areas. So if you just did leg day, use a slower speed with the foam attachment: as it will give you the biggest surface area at the highest effectiveness.

As your muscles start to loosen up, consider raising the speed—finishing with the fastest setting in one location for fifteen to twenty seconds, moving the gun in a circular pattern to break up the scar tissue and knots in your muscles.

A massage gun comes with varying tip-attachments depending on the part of your body you're looking to massage. For example, if you want to massage your back going down your spine, there is a "U" attachment, which is directed at the muscles right next to the spine; or, for the areas that you really want to apply some additional pinpoint pressure to, consider using the "bullet" attachment, as this will absolutely work out those areas of your body very effectively.

18
CONCLUSION

If you've made it this far, you rock. There are people who want to be great, and people who are great because they do the little things right. Finishing this book is one of those little things. It's a true testament to those who want the best from themselves that those people can do what they truly wish as long as they set forth a goal with laser focus and don't stop until they achieve it.

During your kicking and punting journey, you will definitely experience all sorts of highs and lows, but the most important thing remains to not be so hard on yourself. Understand that this is all a beautiful process, and that you can either learn from each situation, good or bad, or allow it to get the best of you and wear you down mentally.

The choice is 100% yours. So make the decision today to be in control of yourself, your mindset, and your life. You are elite as long as YOU believe you are. With this new knowledge, take it and apply it. I would love it if you sent me a message via my email or any social media platform to tell me how much this book has improved your life. You guys are my why, and seeing you guys improve through the lessons and teachings that I've shared is what motivates me every day to continue to help the football kicker world.

Thank you guys so much for reading and we'll talk soon. Until next time,

Eric

19
REFERENCES

Akagi, A. L. (2010, October 20). *About functional strength training.* About Functional Strength Training - Precor (US). https://www.precor.com/en-us/keep-me-moving/articles/about-functional-strength-training.

"Journaling for Mental Health." *Content - Health Encyclopedia - University of Rochester Medical Center,* www.urmc.rochester.edu/encyclopedia/content.aspx?ContentID=4552.

BONUS

This next section is a kicking journal designed by Kickers of earth for you guys to use Fill out each page to track your performance. Over time, you will see a consistent pattern of what you are strong in and what needs work. There will also be a correlation between your mentality and performance so it's important to get into a state of mind to perform at your best level. Use this journal and you will see tangible improvements over time. The following 10 pages are a sample of the Kickers of Earth's Kicking Journal which is available online at kickersofearth.com/journal

Date _____ ☆☆☆☆☆

Weather ☀️ ⛅ ☁️ 🌧️ 🌫️   Temperature _____

What are you working on today? _____
_____
_____
_____

Field Goals

#	Distance	Hash	Result
1			
2			
3			
4			
5			
6			
7			
8			
9			
10			
		Total result	

Kickoffs

#	Distance	Hang Time	Result
1			
2			
3			
4			
5			
6			
7			
8			
9			
10			
Avg.			

Punts

#	Yard line	Hang Time	Get-off time	Distance	Result
1					
2					
3					
4					
5					
6					
7					
8					
9					
10					
Avg.					

How do you feel after the session? _____

What was the most helpful or limiting thing you experienced today? _____
_____

Notes: _____
_____
_____

Date _____
Weather ☼ ⛅ ☁ 🌧 ⛈   Temperature _____
☆☆☆☆☆
What are you working on today? _____
_____
_____

#	Field Goals		
	Distance	Hash	Result
1			
2			
3			
4			
5			
6			
7			
8			
9			
10			
		Total result	

#	Kickoffs		
	Distance	Hang Time	Result
1			
2			
3			
4			
5			
6			
7			
8			
9			
10			
Avg.			

#	Punts			
	Yard line	Hang Time	Get-off time	Distance	Result
1					
2					
3					
4					
5					
6					
7					
8					
9					
10					
Avg.					

How do you feel after the session? _____
_____

What was the most helpful or limiting thing you experienced today? _____
_____

Notes: _____
_____
_____

Date _____ ☆☆☆☆☆

Weather ☀️ ⛅ ☁️ 🌧️ 🌫️ Temperature _____

What are you working on today? _____
_____
_____

Field Goals

#	Distance	Hash	Result
1			
2			
3			
4			
5			
6			
7			
8			
9			
10			
		Total result	

Kickoffs

#	Distance	Hang Time	Result
1			
2			
3			
4			
5			
6			
7			
8			
9			
10			
Avg.			

Punts

#	Yard line	Hang Time	Get-off time	Distance	Result
1					
2					
3					
4					
5					
6					
7					
8					
9					
10					
Avg.					

How do you feel after the session? _____

What was the most helpful or limiting thing you experienced today? _____
_____

Notes: _____
_____
_____

Date _____ ☆☆☆☆☆

Weather ☀ ⛅ ☁ 🌧 ☁   Temperature _____

What are you working on today? _____
_____
_____
_____

Field Goals

#	Distance	Hash	Result
1			
2			
3			
4			
5			
6			
7			
8			
9			
10			
		Total result	

Kickoffs

#	Distance	Hang Time	Result
1			
2			
3			
4			
5			
6			
7			
8			
9			
10			
Avg.			

Punts

#	Yard line	Hang Time	Get-off time	Distance	Result
1					
2					
3					
4					
5					
6					
7					
8					
9					
10					
Avg.					

How do you feel after the session? _____
_____

What was the most helpful or limiting thing you experienced today? _____
_____

Notes: _____
_____
_____

Date _____ ☆☆☆☆☆

Weather ☀ ⛅ ☁ ☁ 🌧 Temperature _____

What are you working on today? _____
_____
_____

Field Goals

#	Distance	Hash	Result
1			
2			
3			
4			
5			
6			
7			
8			
9			
10			
		Total result	

Kickoffs

#	Distance	Hang Time	Result
1			
2			
3			
4			
5			
6			
7			
8			
9			
10			
Avg.			

Punts

#	Yard line	Hang Time	Get-off time	Distance	Result
1					
2					
3					
4					
5					
6					
7					
8					
9					
10					
Avg.					

How do you feel after the session? _____

What was the most helpful or limiting thing you experienced today? _____
_____

Notes: _____
_____
_____

Date _____

Weather ☀ ⛅ ☁ 🌧 🌦 Temperature _____

☆☆☆☆☆

What are you working on today? _____
_____
_____

Field Goals

#	Distance	Hash	Result
1			
2			
3			
4			
5			
6			
7			
8			
9			
10			
		Total result	

Kickoffs

#	Distance	Hang Time	Result
1			
2			
3			
4			
5			
6			
7			
8			
9			
10			
Avg.			

Punts

#	Yard line	Hang Time	Get-off time	Distance	Result
1					
2					
3					
4					
5					
6					
7					
8					
9					
10					
Avg.					

How do you feel after the session? _____
_____

What was the most helpful or limiting thing you experienced today? _____
_____
_____

Notes: _____
_____
_____

Date _____ ☆☆☆☆☆

Weather ☀️ ⛅ ☁️ 🌧️ 🌫️ Temperature _____

What are you working on today? _____
_____
_____

Field Goals

#	Distance	Hash	Result
1			
2			
3			
4			
5			
6			
7			
8			
9			
10			
		Total result	

Kickoffs

#	Distance	Hang Time	Result
1			
2			
3			
4			
5			
6			
7			
8			
9			
10			
Avg.			

Punts

#	Yard line	Hang Time	Get-off time	Distance	Result
1					
2					
3					
4					
5					
6					
7					
8					
9					
10					
Avg.					

How do you feel after the session? _____
_____

What was the most helpful or limiting thing you experienced today? _____
_____
_____

Notes: _____
_____
_____

Date _____   ☆☆☆☆☆

Weather ☀ ⛅ ☁ 🌧 ☁   Temperature _____

What are you working on today? _____
_____
_____

Field Goals

#	Distance	Hash	Result
1			
2			
3			
4			
5			
6			
7			
8			
9			
10			
		Total result	

Kickoffs

#	Distance	Hang Time	Result
1			
2			
3			
4			
5			
6			
7			
8			
9			
10			
Avg.			

Punts

#	Yard line	Hang Time	Get-off time	Distance	Result
1					
2					
3					
4					
5					
6					
7					
8					
9					
10					
Avg.					

How do you feel after the session? _____

What was the most helpful or limiting thing you experienced today? _____
_____

Notes: _____
_____
_____

Date _____ ☆☆☆☆☆

Weather ☀ ⛅ ☁ 🌧 🌦 Temperature _____

What are you working on today? _____
_____
_____

Field Goals

#	Distance	Hash	Result
1			
2			
3			
4			
5			
6			
7			
8			
9			
10			
		Total result	

Kickoffs

#	Distance	Hang Time	Result
1			
2			
3			
4			
5			
6			
7			
8			
9			
10			
Avg.			

Punts

#	Yard line	Hang Time	Get-off time	Distance	Result
1					
2					
3					
4					
5					
6					
7					
8					
9					
10					
Avg.					

How do you feel after the session? _____

What was the most helpful or limiting thing you experienced today? _____
_____

Notes: _____
_____
_____

www.ingramcontent.com/pod-product-compliance
Lightning Source LLC
Chambersburg PA
CBHW072149100526
44589CB00015B/2155